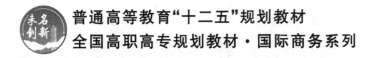

普通高等教育"十二五"规划教材

全国高职高专规划教材·国际商务系列

卖场商品销售英语

English for Commodity Sales in Retail Marketing

刘大为 刘 玥 主编

内 容 简 介

《卖场商品销售英语》主要是针对高等职业院校培养具有熟练英语营销能力的卖场一线销售人员而编写的教材。本教材共分 8 个学习情境，分别是在商业大街上，在百货大楼的化妆品区、服装区、酒水区、副食区、家电区、皮具区、珠宝区购物。以上 8 个学习情境以一对外国夫妇在百货大楼购物的活动为主线串联起来，8 个学习情境中涉及各种卖场销售人员在实际工作中经常遇到的场景，具体包括：引导招呼顾客、询问顾客需求、推荐介绍商品、讨价还价、介绍卖场促销方式、说明付款方式、说明商品售后服务、处理顾客退换货、处理顾客投诉、说明卖场布局、说明营业时间、介绍卖场各种服务（如订制衣服服务、广播失物、送货服务）等。通过以上内容的学习，引导学生熟练掌握商业服务业方面的常用英语。

本教材可供高职国际贸易等专业使用，也可供具备一定英语基础的卖场一线销售人员及其相关服务人员自学或作为培训材料。

图书在版编目(CIP)数据

卖场商品销售英语/刘大为，刘玥主编.—北京：北京大学出版社，2012.8
（全国高职高专规划教材·国际商务系列）
ISBN 978-7-301-20801-4

Ⅰ.①卖… Ⅱ.①刘…②刘… Ⅲ.①销售—英语—高等职业教育—教材 Ⅳ.①H31

中国版本图书馆 CIP 数据核字(2012)第 127712 号

书　　　名：	卖场商品销售英语
著作责任者：	刘大为　刘　玥　主编
策 划 编 辑：	温丹丹
责 任 编 辑：	温丹丹
标 准 书 号：	ISBN 978-7-301-20801-4
出 版 发 行：	北京大学出版社
地　　　址：	北京市海淀区成府路 205 号　100871
网　　　址：	http://www.pup.cn
电 子 邮 箱：	编辑部 zyjy@pup.cn　总编室 zpup@pup.cn
电　　　话：	邮购部 010-62752015　发行部 010-62750672　编辑部 010-62756923
印 刷 者：	北京虎彩文化传播有限公司
经 销 者：	新华书店
	787 毫米×1092 毫米　16 开本　7.75 印张　148 千字
	2012 年 8 月第 1 版　2025 年 2 月第 4 次印刷
定　　　价：	22.00 元

未经许可，不得以任何方式复制或抄袭本书之部分或全部内容。
版权所有，侵权必究
举报电话：010-62752024　电子邮箱：fd@pup.cn
图书如有印装质量问题，请与出版部联系，电话：010-62756370

前 言
Preface

　　《卖场商品销售英语》是针对高等职业院校培养具有熟练英语营销能力的卖场一线销售人员而编写的教材。为了实现"以学生为主体，以就业为导向，以能力为本位，以促进学生可持续发展为目标"的教学理念，本教材在内容编排上改变了大部分传统英语教材通常采用的编写模式，即首先为学生呈现词汇、句子、对话，再以补全对话、翻译、写作等形式加强学生对所学内容的掌握。多年的教学实践显示，在这种传统的教材编写模式下，学生通常会被动地记忆或学习英语词汇、句子与对话，再根据这些内容进行补全对话、翻译、写作等形式的练习。这种方式容易造成学生被动的学习习惯，进而影响学生对所学内容的掌握。为改变这一状况，本教材尝试"以情景模拟为载体、以工作任务为核心"的原则，以提高学生的英语口语能力、主动学习能力、合作能力等为目的，在内容编排与结构设计上突出以下特点。

　　1. 在教材整体内容设计上，以一对外国夫妇在中国某城市购物的活动为主线，设置了这对夫妇在卖场购买化妆品、服装、家电等8个学习情境，这8个学习情境中涉及引导招呼顾客、推荐介绍商品、讨价还价、介绍卖场促销方式、说明付款方式、处理顾客退换货、介绍卖场各种服务等各种卖场销售人员在实际工作中经常遇到的场景，从而引导学生掌握商业服务业方面的常用英语。

　　2. 在内容编排与教学设计上，首先通过为学生呈现学习目标、学习任务、学习材料的形式，让学生明确在每个学习情境下需要达成的学习目标与需要完成的学习任务；再通过学生分组的形式，引导学生根据教材中提出的学习任务，小组协作完成；同时，为了督促学生的主动学习，教材中专门增加了学生小组活动记录与评价部分。学生小组活动记录用来引导学生记录小组成员分工、记录学生自己搜集的学习材料及最终的学习成果（情境对话）；评价部分则主要从教师评价、他人评价、自我评价等不同角度引导学生反思自己的学习活动，从而使教师及学生更好地实现对学习活动的过程性评价。

　　同时，教材中根据相关学习情境的具体内容，针对性地为学生提供了英文形式的卖场布局图、产品说明书、价签等来源于现实生活的学习材料，旨在引导学生学会"发现"生活中随处可见的英语材料，培养学生将英语学习融入日常生活的意识。

3. 在教学方法的设计上，建议教师引导学生根据教材中的学习任务，通过查询英语工具书、向同学或教师请教、收集网络信息等各种形式，以小组形式协作地主动完成对相关词汇与句子的学习。同时，引导小组学生根据教材提供的学习材料以及自己搜集的材料，分组自编情境对话，并进行情景剧表演。这种教学方法的设计，旨在培养学生主动学习的习惯，提高学生自学英语的能力，以及信息查询、信息积累、小组合作等各种方法与社会能力。

因此，本教材也可以说是一本学生活动手册，通过以上形式的内容编排、结构设计与教学活动安排，引导学生在主动的"做"中"学"英语，并在"学"中反思、评价自己的学习过程，养成主动学习、积极思考的学习习惯。而教师则应更多地扮演引导者的角色，在学生分组、任务完成及评价等过程中给予更多指导与帮助，推动学生完成学习任务。

本教材共有8个学习情境，建议每个学习情境6个学时，共48个学时。在每个学习情境中，建议前4个学时引导学生掌握学习材料，并为自编情境对话搜集相关材料；后2个学时引导学生自编情境对话、完成情景剧表演，并对学生的学习活动进行评价。

音频资料

本教材配有每个学习情境中相关单词与句子部分的翻译及可供参考的情境对话。同时，单词、句子与参考对话配有录音，由美籍专业人士录制，语音纯正，便于模仿。读者可以用微信扫描左侧的二维码获取学习资料。

本教材由北京财贸职业学院国际教育学院教师刘大为与刘玥共同完成，刘大为负责教材整体设计及最后的定稿。其中，学习情境1～4由刘大为负责，学习情境5～8由刘玥负责。同时，感谢北京财贸职业学院科研处处长田志英副教授为本教材的整体设计思路提出的宝贵意见与建议。

本教材在编写过程中，还参阅了大量相关资料，在此对作者一并表示衷心的感谢！尽管我们力图在本教材的内容编排、教学设计方面有所突破，但由于能力与水平有限，不当之处还望读者指正。

编者
2025年2月修订

目 录
Contents

Scene One	In the Wangfujing Street	1
Scene Two	At the Cosmetics Area	11
Scene Three	At the Men's and Women's Wear Area	21
Scene Four	At the Liquor Area	31
Scene Five	At the Grocery Area	41
Scene Six	At the Home Appliance Area	51
Scene Seven	At the Leather Goods Area	61
Scene Eight	At the Gold and Jewelry Area	71
Keys		81
Bibliography		117

Scene One
In the Wangfujing Street

学习目标		
专业能力	方法能力	社会能力
●能用英语简单介绍王府井商业大街及北京市百货大楼； ●能读懂英文商场布局图并能用英语说出商场销售的各种常见商品种类； ●作为商场服务台人员，能够简单回答顾客对商场相关信息的提问； ●能用所给材料及查找的信息按照要求自编英语对话； ●能够按照自编对话自然地进行情景剧表演。	●能利用互联网、英语字典、书籍等各种方式查找需要的信息； ●逐步培养整合并积累信息的学习习惯。	●能自行完成小组成员的任务分工并共同完成任务； ●能接受他人的合理意见； ●能清晰地表达自己的意见并说服他人接受自己的意见； ●能对他人及自己进行客观真实的评价。
学习任务		
●根据提供的场景描述及相关材料，每个小组合作完成讨论王府井商业大街及北京市百货大楼的情境对话，并进行情景剧表演； ●情境对话中要包含场景描述中提到的内容，同时每个小组可根据需要适当增加情节； ●情境对话中的人物可根据情节需要自行增加或减少。		

卖场商品销售英语

Information Bank

Scene description

Linda陪同来自国外的客户Green夫妇逛王府井商业大街，Green夫妇对王府井商业大街的繁华早有耳闻，对其非常感兴趣。他们不停地向Linda询问关于王府井商业大街的各种问题，诸如其名称的来历、商业的发展及其各种商场的分布等信息。Linda耐心地回答他们的问题，并提议他们可以到北京市百货大楼去购物，同时也为他们简单介绍了北京市百货大楼的基本情况。在百货大楼里，他们先到总服务台拿了一本购物指南，并向服务台工作人员简单询问了百货大楼提供的服务、购物等方面的信息。

Roles

Linda
Mrs. Green
Mr. Green
receptionist

Related words and expressions

Useful words and phrases

1. cosmetics	n.		化妆品
2. superstore	n.		超级商场
3. souvenirs	n.		纪念品
4. fair	n.		集市
5. elevator	n.		电梯
6. boutique	n.		精品店
7. lingerie	n.		女士内衣
8. stall	n.		摊位，铺子，售货亭
9. supermarket	n.		超市
10. store	n.		商店
11. escalator / moving staircase	n.		扶梯
12. establish	v.		建立，成立
13. large-scale	adj.		大型的
14. mansion	n.		宅邸，大厦
15. the cashier's			收银处
16. E-commerce			电子商务
17. household supplies			家居装饰

Scene One In the Wangfujing Street

18. free mobile phone battery charging — 手机免费充电
19. traditional shopping way — 传统购物方式
20. free delivery — 免费送货服务
21. lift lobby — 电梯厅
22. handbags & accessories — 手袋饰品
23. window shopper — 只逛不买的人
24. clock & eyewear — 钟表眼镜
25. store layout — 楼层分布图
26. general enquiry — 询问服务
27. specialty shop — 专卖店，专营商店
28. pedestrian street — 步行街
29. cyber ordering — 网络订购
30. digital products — 数码产品
31. Beijing specialties — 北京特产
32. VIP center — 会员中心
33. free alteration — 免费（衣服）修改服务
34. men's suits — 男士正装
35. free parking — 免费停车服务
36. shopping mania — 购物狂
37. commercial centre — 商业中心
38. information center, service desk, reception desk — （商场的）服务台
39. group buying/ group purchase — 团购
40. men's casual wear — 休闲男装
41. department store — 大商场
42. gold & jewelry — 黄金珠宝
43. return and exchange — 退换货服务
44. China Time-honored Brand — 中华老字号
45. women's luxury wear — 成熟女装
46. public phone — 公用电话
47. fan store — 爱好者商店
48. camera & video equipment — 照摄器材
49. bargain seeker — 专买打折产品的人
50. public announcement — 广播寻人服务
51. shopping guide — 购物指南
52. tobaccos, liquor & tea — 烟酒茶叶
53. shopping centre — 购物中心
54. free gift packing — 免费礼品包装服务

3

55. knitted underwear	针织内衣
56. electric appliance	家用电器
57. shopping mall	综合性购物中心
58. long-established shop	百年老店
59. shopping plaza	购物广场
60. sensible shopper	理智消费者
61. office supplies	办公用品
62. flea market	跳蚤市场
63. lost and found office	（商场的）失物认领处
64. come into being	形成，产生
65. daily necessities	日用品，生活必需品

Useful expressions

1. Beijing Department store is divided into north wing and south wing.

2. Thank you. You're so helpful.

3. The Wangfujing area is in the heart of Beijing, next to the Forbidden City, and Tian'anmen Square.

4. Since Dong'an Market was established in 1903, the Wangfujing Street has become a commercial centre in Beijing.

5. Please go ahead and take the escalator.

6. Wangfujing Street is famous for the long-established shops such as the silks of Ruifuxiang, the scissors of Wangmazi, the roast ducks of Quanjude, the shoes of Neiliansheng and Buyingzhai, and so on.

7. What time do you open / close tomorrow?

8. The main shops in the Wangfujing Street are Oriental Plaza, Beijing Department Store, Foreign Language Bookstore, Danyao Building, Gongmei Building, Wangfu Women Department Store, Moslem Building, Xin Dong An Plaza, etc..

9. There are more than 200 shops on the 810 meter-long Pedestrian Street from Nankou of Wangfujing to Goldfish Kou.

10. Does the elevator stop on the fourth floor?

11. Founded in 1955, Beijing Department Store is the first large-scale shopping mall in Beijing after New China was established in 1949.

12. The street came into being in the Yuan Dynasty more than 700 years ago. In the Ming Dynasty, one of the emperors built 10 mansions for his 10 brothers in this street, and the street was then named Shiwangfu, meaning mansions for 10 imperial brothers. In 1915, the government renamed the street as Wangfujing Street, for there is a sweet-water well on the south part of the street.

Scene One In the Wangfujing Street

13. Is there any public telephone here?
14. Wangfujing Street is congested with large shops, hotels, specialty shops and famous long-established shops. It is the sister street of Champs-Elysees in France.
15. Beijing Department Store has made itself known as the place to easily find daily necessities as well as a place the customer can trust.
16. I've long heard of it.
17. At present, there are five major commercial areas such as Wangfujing area, Xidan commercial area, Dashilanr commercial area, Longfusi commercial area and Chaoyangmenwai commercial area in Beijing.
18. Where can I buy children's wear?
19. In English, the words *Wangfujing* means the Well of the Prince's Mansion.
20. Seeing for oneself is better than hearing from others.
21. May I get a shopping guide here?
22. The Wangfujing Street is well known all over China for its comprehensiveness, fashion, high quality and sophisticated cultural activities.
23. Beijing Department Store was reopened to the public on August 28, 1999 after a five-month-long massive refurbishment.
24. The toilet is around that corner next to the cashier's.
25. After New China was established, the Wangfujing area gradually became the city's landmark commercial centre.
26. Beijing Department Store has a favorable reputation due to its top-notch service and more than 2 000 brands in over 70 000 varieties of goods.
27. Excuse me, where is the reception desk?
28. We offer free mobile phone battery charging service. You can charge your mobile phone here.
29. Thanks for stopping by, sir.
30. We open from 10 a.m. to 10 p.m..

Store layout

	South Wing		North Wing
		8F	Cinema
		7F	Restaurant
		6F	Household Supplies Electric Appliances Office Supplies Camera & Video Equipment Digital Products
5F	Children's Wear and Products Children's Toys	5F	Sportswear Sports Equipment Out-door Goods Casual wear
4F	Men's Leather Goods Men's Shoes	4F	Men's Suits Men's Casual Wear Men's Accessories Out-door Goods
3F	Lingerie Knitted and Cotton Goods	3F	Young Fashion Wear Women's Luxury Wear Accessories
2F	Women's Shoes	2F	Women's Luxury Wear Women's Handbag Accessories Fashion Watches
1F	Cosmetics Luxury Gold & Jewelry Women's Shoes Fabric Shoes	1F	Luxury Jewelry Luxury Watches Women's Handbag STARBUCKS
	北京市百货大楼 Beijing Department Store	B1	Food & Beverages Supermarket Beijing Specialties
		B2	Food & Beverages

(Reference: Layout of Beijing Department Store)

Scene One   In the Wangfujing Street

 Students' Task

Please finish the following tasks according to the given words, phrases, expressions and scene description.

Team work 1

Find out the words and phrases related to shopping place.
Find out the words and phrases related to shopping way.
Find out the words and phrases related to categories of goods.
Find out the words and phrases related to shopping mall facilities.
Find out the words and phrases related to services in the shopping places.
Find out the words and phrases related to consumer type.

Team work 2

Find out the sentences talking about history of Wangfujing Street.
Find out the sentences talking about current situation of Wangfujing Street.
Find out the sentences talking about history of Beijing Department Store.
Find out the sentences talking about the current situation of Beijing Department Store.
Find out the sentences that may happen between customers and salespersons.

Team work 3

Make a conversation according to the given scene description, words and expressions.

Team work 4

Role Play: Act out the above conversation.

Team work record

The members of team

Number	Name	The task of every member	role
1			
2			
3			
4			
...			

Useful words collected

Useful expressions collected

Scene One *In the Wangfujing Street*

Team Fruit (Conversation made according to the scene description)

The evaluation from teacher

The evaluation from other teams

The evaluation from the member of your team

The evaluation from yourself

Scene Two
At the Cosmetics Area

 Objectives

学习目标		
专业能力	方法能力	社会能力
●能说出各类化妆品的英语名称； ●能读懂化妆品产品说明书并能根据说明书用英语简单介绍化妆品的功效、使用方法； ●作为销售人员，能用英语流利地招呼顾客、听不懂时能礼貌地请顾客重复解释、会简单询问顾客需求并向顾客推荐商品； ●能站在顾客角度，用英语表达自己的购买想法、能就商品的相关问题向销售人员提问； ●能用所给材料及自己查找的信息按照要求自编英语对话； ●能够按照自编对话自然地进行情景剧表演。	●能够利用互联网、英语字典、书籍等各种方式查找自己需要的信息； ●能够从各种信息中筛选需要的有用信息； ●能够总结有效的英语学习方法并与同学进行分享。	●能自行完成小组成员的任务分工并共同完成任务； ●能接受他人的合理意见； ●能清晰地表达自己的意见并说服他人接受自己的意见； ●能对他人及自己进行客观真实的评价。
学习任务		

●根据教师提供的场景描述及相关材料，每个小组合作完成情境对话，并进行情景剧表演；
●情境对话中要包含场景描述中提到的内容，同时每个小组可根据需要适当增加情节；
●情境对话中的人物可根据情节需要自行增加或减少。

Information Bank

Scene description 1

在化妆品区，售货员热情地向Green夫妇打招呼，询问他们想要买什么。Mrs. Green表现出对某个化妆品感兴趣，并询问一些关于该品牌的问题，售货员没有听明白，请Mrs. Green再说一遍；Mrs. Green又换了一种比较简单的表述方法，慢慢地重复了一遍。售货员询问Mrs. Green想要买哪种类型的化妆品，如爽肤水、洗面奶、面膜、润肤霜、眼霜还是防晒霜。Mrs. Green表示不知道该品牌是否适合她；售货员通过简单询问她的肤质又向她推荐另一品牌的产品，并简单说明了该产品的功效。

Scene description 2

Mr. Green在化妆品区，售货员热情地向Mr. Green打招呼，询问他想要买什么。Mr. Green想给他夫人买套化妆品作为生日礼物，但他对女士化妆品不是很了解，所以他请Linda帮忙挑选。售货员耐心地向Mr. Green介绍女士化妆品套装产品，Mr. Green问了几个关于化妆品功效的问题。有些问题售货员没有听明白，就请Mr. Green再说一遍。经过一番询问，Mr. Green担心他选的化妆品与夫人的肤质不合适，决定改选香水。售货员向他推荐了一款香水，Mr. Green认为不错并买了下来。

Roles

Shop assistant / salesgirl / salesman / saleswoman / salesclerk
Linda
Mrs. Green
Mr. Green

Related words and expressions

Useful words and phrases

1. puff	n.	粉扑
2. makeup	n.	化妆品
3. lipstick	n.	口红，唇膏
4. nutritious	adj.	滋养的
5. perfume	n.	香水
6. essence	n.	精华液
7. curler	n.	卷发夹
8. exfoliate	v.	去角质

Scene Two At the Cosmetics Area

9. mask	n.	面膜
10. mascara	n.	睫毛膏
11. waterproof	adj.	防水的
12. remover	n.	卸妆水
13. alcohol-free	adj.	不含酒精的
14. blush	n.	腮红
15. cosmetics	n.	化妆品，彩妆
16. anti-wrinkle	adj.	抗老防皱的
17. cleansing lotion		洁肤露
18. normal skin		中性皮肤
19. brow brush		眉刷
20. deep moisturizing cleansing foam		深层保湿洁面乳
21. cotton bud / Q-tips		棉签
22. whitening sunblock lotion		美白防晒乳液
23. sun blocking cream / sun cream		防晒霜
24. firming complex / firming essence		紧肤精华素
25. lip contour pencil / lip liner		唇线笔
26. eye gel		眼霜
27. bath foam		沐浴液
28. oily skin		油性皮肤
29. eye shadow		眼影
30. foundation cream		粉底霜
31. acne skin		痤疮皮肤
32. oil-absorbing sheets		吸油纸
33. nourishing sleeping mask		滋养睡眠面膜
34. pressed powder		粉饼
35. beauty box		化妆盒
36. toning lotion		化妆水，爽肤水
37. night cream		晚霜
38. electric shaver		电动剃须刀
39. purifying toning lotion		净化爽肤水
40. shaving-lotion		剃须膏
41. lip gloss / lip color		唇彩
42. razor blade		（剃须刀的）刀片
43. sensitive skin		敏感性皮肤
44. cleansing milk / cleansing foam / cleanser		洁面乳，洗面奶
45. eye shadow brush / shadow applicator		眼影刷

46. eye mask 眼膜
47. moisturizing lotion / cream 保湿乳/霜
48. dry skin 干性皮肤
49. facial cream 面霜
50. oil-control cream 控油面霜
51. cotton pads 化妆棉
52. combination skin / mixed skin 混合性皮肤
53. eyelash curler 睫毛夹
54. skin care product 护肤品
55. ultraviolet radiation 紫外线

Useful expressions

1. The gentle formula keeps skin soft and healthy.
2. The perfume smells good. I'll buy it.
3. Are you looking for something?
4. You'd better use the purifying toning lotion because of your oily skin.
5. I have combination skin. My T-zone gets oil easily, but my cheeks are dry in the autumn and winter.
6. Pardon? / I beg your pardon? / Pardon me?
7. I have oily skin. My face always breaks out.
8. I want to buy a bottle of whitening sunblock lotion. / I'd like to buy a bottle of whitening sunblock lotion.
9. Do you have firming lotion and facial cream?
10. Would you please show me how to use the eyelash curler?
11. I don't like this flavor.
12. The mask suits for dry skin.
13. The essence is for anti-wrinkling and whitening.
14. Excuse me. What do you mean by *oil-control cream*?
15. I'm looking for a lipstick.
16. What can I do for you? / May I help you? / Good afternoon, madam, something for you? / Can I help you?
17. Would you mind my recommending?
18. How's about this brand? It is a new brand.
19. Don't stick with the same brand of cream for too long.
20. Welcome, sir. Please take you time.
21. The moisturizing lotion is anti-dryness, it can moisturize your skin.
22. I'm sorry. I didn't understand you.

Scene Two *At the Cosmetics Area*

23. I'm just looking around.
24. So many people bought it and it is said that it's not bad.
25. What is for anti-dryness?
26. The lotion smells too strong. I can't stand it.
27. Well. Would you please say it again?
28. Here is the sample. You can have a try.
29. I want to buy a mask. Could you show me one?
30. Everybody is welcome here, madam, whether she buys or not.
31. I'm not sure if this color matches my skin tone. May I have a try?
32. It sounds good, but let me think about it and come back.
33. Well, I'll be back.
34. Would you please recommend some perfume for me?
35. You'd better buy this kind of cleansing milk.
36. Excuse me. I'm afraid I can't say it in English.
37. My facial skin has been very dry these days. Do you have any moisturizing lotion?
38. My skin is very sensitive. It's always allergic to many skin care product.
39. I mean do you sell any kind of perfume without alcohol?
40. Do these products have certificates?
41. I always get rough skin in winter.
42. What's the best brand for night cream?
43. I'd like something that's not too strong. She likes softer smelling perfume.
44. I think your skin is on the oily side, and this one is designed for oily skin.
45. The cleansing foam cleans thoroughly without striping your natural protective oil. The gentle formula keeps skin clean, clear, smooth and soft.
46. Would you please speak more slowly?
47. How about buying a lip gloss? The sparking effect makes you younger.
48. The foundation cream only uses the finest ingredients. It will moisturize your skin and it can protect your skin from harmful ultraviolet radiation.
49. You'd better use a gentler, cream based facial cleanser, and remember to follow that with a thick moisturizer.
50. Do you have any skin care products that can keep my skin soft and super?

Cosmetic instructions

Cleansing Lotion
Especially formulated for sensitive skin, this tissue-off formula contains unique natural ingredients which thoroughly and gently cleanse while rendering special soothing properties for sun burnt skin. The skin becomes clean, clear, smooth and soft.

Application
Apply on dry face with fingertips, using an upward circular motion, and avoid eye area. Remove with cotton pad and rinse off.

Moisture Mask
An instant lift to dull and dehydrated skin, it works to lighten, moisturized and revitalize. In just 15 minutes, the Whitening Essence improves dark spots and freckles caused by UV rays. Soluble Collagen increases suppleness of skin while minerals increase water content of skin cell and its ability to lock moisture.

Application
Apply onto cleaned skin and leave for about 15 minutes. Avoid eye area. Rinse well.

Students' Task

Please finish the following tasks according to the given words, phrases, expressions and scene description.

Team work 1

Find out the words and phrases related to cosmetic products.
Find out the words and phrases related to makeup tools.

Scene Two At the Cosmetics Area

Find out the words and phrases related to type of skin.
Find out the words and phrases related to function of cosmetics.

Team work 2

Find out the sentences used to greet customers and reply from customers.
Find out the sentences used to ask for repeat and its reply.
Find out the sentences used to recommend and introduce products.
Find out the sentences used to express desires of customers and purchasing interests.

Team work 3

Make a conversation according to the given scene description, words and expressions.

Team work 4

Role Play: Act out the above conversation.

 Team work record

The members of team

Number	Name	The task of every member	role
1			
2			
3			
4			
...			

17

卖场商品销售英语

Useful words collected

Useful expressions collected

Team Fruit (Conversation made according to the scene description)

Scene Two *At the Cosmetics Area*

 *Evaluation*

> The evaluation from teacher

> The evaluation from other teams

> The evaluation from the member of your team

> The evaluation from yourself

Scene Three: At the Men's and Women's Wear Area

 Objectives

学习目标		
专业能力	方法能力	社会能力
● 能说出各类衣服的英语名称； ● 作为销售人员，会用英语流利地向顾客介绍服装的材质、价格、款式等，会根据顾客实际情况向顾客推荐适合的衣服，并能说服顾客购买商品； ● 作为销售人员，会用英语表达库存信息，说明商场定做衣服的服务； ● 能站在顾客角度，用英语表达自己对商品的看法，并会委婉拒绝销售人员的推销； ● 能用所给材料及自己查找的信息按照要求自编英语对话； ● 能够按照自编对话自然地进行情景剧表演。	● 能够利用互联网、英语字典、书籍等各种方式查找自己需要的信息； ● 能够从各种信息中筛选需要的有用信息； ● 能够总结有效的英语学习方法并与同学进行分享。	● 能自行完成小组成员的任务分工并共同完成任务； ● 能接受他人的合理意见； ● 能清晰地表达自己的意见并说服他人接受自己的意见； ● 能对他人及自己进行客观真实的评价。
学习任务		

● 根据教师提供的场景描述及相关材料，每个小组合作完成情境对话，并进行情景剧表演；
● 情境对话中要包含场景描述中提到的内容，同时每个小组可根据需要适当增加情节；
● 情境对话中的人物可根据情节需要自行增加或减少。

Information Bank

Scene description 1

在男士服装区，售货员向Green夫妇热情打招呼，询问Green夫妇喜欢什么款式的衣服，Mr. Green看上一件衣服（如男士夹克、男士风衣或男士西服等）。在Green夫妇的询问下，售货员向他们耐心介绍了衣服的品牌、价格、材质、保养、质量等问题。Mr. Green认为衣服的材质不错，但是价格似乎有点贵。售货员说明这款衣服是今年的流行款式，并建议Mr. Green试穿一下。Mr. Green试穿后，觉得不太合适，就委婉拒绝了售货员的推销。

Scene description 2

在女士服装区，Mrs. Green看中了一套中式旗袍，售货员向她介绍了旗袍的材质，如说明旗袍是用上等的苏杭丝绸做成，穿起来感觉很舒适，并说明其做工很精致，上面的花纹很有中国特色，同时款式又比较符合西方人的体型。Mrs. Green试穿后觉得旗袍有点紧，要求换一件大一号的再试穿一下，但是售货员发现店里大一号的旗袍没有Mrs. Green喜欢的颜色了。售货员查库存后，非常抱歉地告诉Mrs. Green库存中也没有她喜欢的颜色的大号旗袍。这让Mrs. Green感到很惋惜，因为她的确非常喜欢这件旗袍。于是，售货员建议她定做一件旗袍，并简单介绍了商场定做旗袍的相关服务。

Roles

Shop assistant / salesgirl / salesman / saleswoman / salesclerk
Linda
Mrs. Green
Mr. Green

Related words and expressions

Useful words and phrases

1. material	n.	材质，质地
2. slack	adj.	（衣服）宽松的
3. style	n.	款式
4. jacket	n.	夹克
5. sleeveless	adj.	无袖的
6. light	adj.	（颜色）浅的
7. stock	n.	库存，存货

Scene Three At the Men's and Women's Wear Area

8. sportswear	n.	运动装
9. wool	n.	羊毛
10. design	n.	设计
11. beige	n., adj.	米色；米色的
12. small (S)	adj.	（衣服）小号的
13. stripe	n.	条纹，线条
14. silk	n.	丝绸
15. collarless	adj.	无领的
16. catalogue	n.	目录，货物价目表
17. close-fitting	adj.	贴身的，紧身的
18. medium (M)	adj.	（衣服）中号的
19. rayon	n.	人造丝
20. tailor-made	adj.	定做
21. tight	adj.	（衣服）紧的
22. size	n.	尺寸，型号
23. velvet	n.	丝绒
24. purple	n., adj.	紫色；紫色的
25. embroidery	n.	绣花，刺绣
26. chiffon	n.	雪纺绸
27. large (L)	adj.	（衣服）大号的
28. flounce	n.	荷叶边
29. fade	v.	褪色
30. star	n.	星点花，星型图案
31. linen	n.	亚麻
32. overcoat	n.	大衣
33. fit / suit	v.	合身
34. durable	adj.	耐穿的
35. frock	n.	连衣裙
36. brand	n.	商标，牌子
37. shrink-proof	adj.	防缩水的
38. cashmere	n.	山羊绒，开司米
39. suits	n.	西服（套装）
40. dry-cleaned	adj.	干洗的
41. mink	n.	貂皮
42. pattern	n.	花样，图案
43. dark	adj.	（颜色）深的
44. line	n.	纹路

45. pullover	n.	套头毛衣，套衫
46. pants	n.	裤子
47. casual wear		休闲装
48. cotton fabric		棉织品
49. printed pattern		印花
50. extra large (XL)		（衣服）加大号的
51. plain satin		素缎
52. Chinese-style long gown / Chi-pao		旗袍
53. fits like a glove		非常合身
54. fitting room		试衣间
55. fur coat		毛外套
56. figured satin		花缎
57. formal suit		正装
58. machine washable		可以机洗的
59. man-made fiber		人造纤维
60. woolen sweater		羊毛衫
61. coin dots		大圆点花
62. milk white		乳白色
63. dress coat		小礼服
64. price tag		价签
65. block plaid		大方格
66. bell-bottomed trousers		喇叭裤
67. pin dots		小圆点花
68. man-made leather		人造革
69. lattice check		小方格
70. business suit		职业装

Useful expressions

1. Do you sell fur coat here?

2. You've talked me into buying this frock.

3. I'm afraid it's too narrow across the shoulders and a little short in the sleeves. Do you have a larger one?

4. This leather jacket suits you well. It goes very well with your jeans.

5. Will the color fade?

6. The skirt is a little bit too revealing.

7. I need a dress for a wedding ceremony. Which do you think suit me better?

Scene Three At the Men's and Women's Wear Area

8. This close-fitting dress looks elegant on you. Perhaps it's the cutting that makes you feel tight. Frankly speaking, not many people could wear this kind of style well. You're one of the exceptions.
9. It's the latest fashion, very popular.
10. Well, it's a bit tight.
11. What brand is this suit?
12. You look very nice on this overcoat.
13. What's the price for the suits? / How much is the suits? / How much is the suits worth? / How much do you charge for the suits?
14. I think double breasted suit is better than single breasted suit.
15. The fitting room is over there.
16. I can't remember my waist measurement, but I can try it on, can't I?
17. I'm afraid the size L for the yellow Chi-paos are sold out.
18. What style do you prefer, fashionable or conservative?
19. Would you mind I recommend this one? Its design is very elegant.
20. Where are the dresses that were advertised for 20 percent off?
21. These patterns come in different colors and sizes.
22. It's a bit loose. Do you have size in the middle?
23. Something is wrong with the zipper of this sports coat.
24. How do I look in this new overcoat?
25. Please come to the tailoring department with me. They will take your measurements.
26. Please show me the yellow jacket that is hanging over there.
27. What kind of material are the pants made of?
28. The design of our Chi-pao is very elegant, and the patterns are very Chinese.
29. The color seems a little too bright for me.
30. The design and the material are quite OK, but the color doesn't suit me.
31. If this white skirt had a petticoat, I would take it.
32. I prefer a V-shaped collar to a turtleneck.
33. We have alternation service, and it's free.
34. They spend 50 Yuan for this dress coat.
35. The material is washable and will not shrink or fade any more.
36. How about the handiwork?
37. Some of our Chi-paos are specially designed for foreigners with tall figures.
38. Are these coats on sale?
39. How should I wash this woolen sweater?
40. The Jeans need to be taken off about an inch.
41. Will it shrink after being washed / after I wash it?

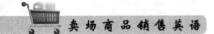

42. The color of your tie doesn't go well with the suit. I suggest you try the black or dark gray ones.
43. Would you consider a tailor-made a Chi-pao? It costs more or less the same as the ready-made one. But they are much fitted to the body, and are much more carefully finished.
44. Does this dress come in any other color or size? I need extra large size.
45. The pure woolen suits must be dry-cleaned.
46. Is this skirt in style / in fashion?
47. It feels a little tight around the waist.
48. What a large variety of coats here! I really don't know which one to choose.
49. I want to buy a black suit. May I try this suit on?
50. I like the design and material, but not the price.
51. I don't think gray suits me well. It's too dull for me.
52. Is it machine-washable?
53. Will this coat keep me warm?
54. What size do you want?
55. Let me check the stock.

Price Tag

Retail price	
RMB	SN.
Product Name	Unit
Place of production	Class
Specification	Complaints Hotline

Supervised No. Zou-8
Price Complaints Hotline: 12358

Scene Three   *At the Men's and Women's Wear Area*

 Students' Task

Please finish the following tasks according to the given words, phrases, expressions and scene description.

Team work 1

Find out the words and phrases related to types of clothes.
Find out the words and phrases related to material of clothes.
Find out the words and phrases related to style of clothes.
Find out the words and phrases related to color of clothes.
Find out the words and phrases related to size of clothes.
Find out the words and phrases related to pattern of clothes.
Find out the words and phrases related to quality of material.

Team work 2

Find out the sentences used to express purchasing interests and desires of customers.
Find out the sentences used to recommend goods.
Find out the sentences used to try on clothes.
Find out the sentences used to ask and answer the material, style, workmanship, pattern, color, size, quality, maintenance of the clothes.
Find out the sentences used to express if to buy or not.

Team work 3

Make a conversation according to the given scene description, words and expressions.

Team work 4

Role Play: Act out the above conversation.

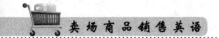

 Team work record

The members of team

Number	Name	The task of every member	role
1			
2			
3			
4			
...			

Useful words collected

Useful expressions collected

Scene Three At the Men's and Women's Wear Area

Team Fruit (Conversation made according to the scene description)

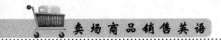

 *Evaluation*

The evaluation from teacher

The evaluation from other teams

The evaluation from the member of your team

The evaluation from yourself

Scene Four

At the Liquor Area

 Objectives

学习目标		
专业能力	方法能力	社会能力
●能说出各种酒类的英语名称； ●能读懂葡萄酒英文说明书； ●能用英语简单介绍葡萄酒的特点、功效等； ●作为销售人员，会用英语流利地向顾客介绍商场的促销方式； ●能站在顾客角度，用英语与销售人员进行讨价还价； ●能用所给材料及自己查找的信息按照要求自编英语对话； ●能够按照自编对话自然地进行情景剧表演。	●能够利用互联网、英语字典、书籍等各种方式查找自己需要的信息； ●能够从各种信息中筛选需要的有用信息； ●能够总结有效的英语学习方法并与同学进行分享。	●能自行完成小组成员的任务分工并共同完成任务； ●能接受他人的合理意见； ●能清晰地表达自己的意见并说服他人接受自己的意见； ●能对他人及自己进行客观真实的评价。
学习任务		

●根据教师提供的场景描述及相关材料，每个小组合作完成情境对话，并进行情景剧表演；
●情境对话中要包含场景描述中提到的内容，同时每个小组可根据需要适当增加情节；
●情境对话中的人物可根据情节需要自行增加或减少。

Information Bank

Scene description

Mr. Green想给朋友买一些中国酒。在商场的酒水区，售货员热情地向他们打招呼。Mr. Green说明想买中国酒送给本国的朋友。于是，售货员向他介绍了中国几种比较著名的白酒和葡萄酒。听完介绍后，Mr. Green选择了购买葡萄酒。售货员向他推荐长城牌葡萄酒，并说明该葡萄酒在国内是大众喜欢的品牌。Mr. Green想多买一些葡萄酒，希望售货员在价格上能给予优惠。售货员指出，现在顾客购买葡萄酒有三种优惠可以享受：（1）葡萄酒买2赠1（1小瓶），并送瓶启一个；（2）如果持有王府井百货大楼的会员卡，可以在总价基础上再打9折；（3）在烟酒专柜消费300元以上，即可参加商场的抽奖活动。Linda恰好有该商场的会员卡，可以借给Mr. Green。Mr. Green认为商场的促销活动很划算，于是决定购买葡萄酒。

Roles

Shop assistant / salesgirl / salesman / saleswoman / salesclerk
Linda
Mrs. Green
Mr. Green

Related words and expressions

Useful words and phrases

1. liquor	n.	酒；烈性酒	
2. bouquet	n.	酒香	
3. wine	n.	葡萄酒	
4. spirits	n.	（常做复数）烈酒；酒精，乙醇	
5. mellow	adj.	醇美的，醇香的	
6. quality	n.	质量	
7. vintage	n.	一个收获季节采得的葡萄所酿制的酒	
8. giveaway	n.	赠品	
9. sorghum	n.	高粱	
10. installment	n.	分期付款	
11. beer	n.	啤酒	
12. quantity	n.	数量	
13. raffle	n.	抽彩，抽奖	
14. aroma	n.	果香	

Scene Four At the Liquor Area

15. discount	*v., n.*	折扣
16. cocktail	*n.*	鸡尾酒
17. strong	*adj.*	（酒性）烈性的
18. wheat	*n.*	小麦
19. mild	*adj.*	淡的，不浓的
20. cork	*n.*	软木塞
21. scent	*n.*	植物香气
22. afford	*v.*	买得起
23. corkscrew	*n.*	开瓶器
24. overcharge	*v.*	要价太高
25. coupon	*n.*	优惠券
26. alcohol	*n.*	酒，含酒精的饮料；酒精，乙醇
27. barley	*n.*	大麦
28. champagne	*n.*	香槟酒
29. bargain	*v., n.*	讨价还价
30. grape	*n.*	葡萄
31. 10% off		九折
32. on sale		特价销售
33. a fair deal		公平交易
34. cost price		成本价
35. go to head		（酒）上头
36. red wine		红葡萄酒
37. bottom price		底价，最低价
38. membership card		会员卡
39. rose wine		玫瑰红葡萄酒
40. ceiling price		最高价
41. white wine		白葡萄酒
42. special price		特价
43. dry wine		干葡萄酒
44. gift coupon		礼券
45. sweet wine		甜葡萄酒
46. knock off		减价
47. draught beer		生啤
48. wine preserved for years		陈年葡萄酒
49. rice wine		米酒
50. price reduction		减价
51. reasonable price		价格合理，价格公道

52. pay by cash / credit card   通过现金 / 信用卡支付
53. yellow rice wine   黄酒
54. net price   实价
55. sticky rice   糯米

Useful expressions

1. Can you give me a better price?

2. Moutai is one of the most famous liquors in China. It tastes good indeed.

3. The price is reasonable because the quality is super.

4. Do you accept / take credit card?

5. That's the lowest price. / That's the bottom price.

6. We offer a nice free gift for every purchase over 100 dollars.

7. We can't make any reductions. It's our store rule.

8. That's too expensive. You're robbing me!

9. The older a wine gets, the better it is.

10. As far as the quality is concerned, it is worth the price.

11. How is the bouquet of the wine?

12. We're on clearance sale now. Prices have up to 20 percent off. Do not miss the chance.

13. It's rather strong, but never goes to head.

14. Since you are coming to us for the first time, I'll take off ten percent from the price on the tag. You can't be wrong on that price.

15. We sell mild wines and strong liquors.

16. Is it true that imported wines are better than domestic?

17. This brandy has a fine bouquet.

18. Chinese white spirit is made from barley, wheat or Chinese sorghum, while the Chinese rice wine is made from rice or sticky rice.

19. I can't buy with your price.

20. Many people in the north are fond of liquor. I think it has something to do with the climate.

21. Make me an offer.

22. Moutai liquor is regarded as China's national liquor. It's often a must for a grand banquet.

23. I'll be buying more, couldn't you knock off a little bit more?

24. We are practically giving this away. It's almost the cost price.

25. The wine is characterized by its intense scent of blackberries. It has a soft finish, supported by a low tannin content.

Scene Four *At the Liquor Area*

26. You can buy it by installment plan.
27. This wine goes very well with sea-fish.
28. Show me the best champagne in your counter, please.
29. It's a square dealing.
30. This medium-dry sparkling wine is fruity and rich. It contains fruit's acidity and the light feeling in the mouth, makes the association of bitter almond's fragrance.
31. Riesling is a white grape variety originating in the Rhine region of Germany. It is typically used to make dry, semi-sweet, sweet and sparkling white wines.
32. This Riesling captivates everyone with its youthfully fresh interplay of aromas: ripe citrus fruits, coupled with juicy peaches.
33. It's a well-known kind of wine in China. It tastes good.
34. There will be a luck raffle draw. First prize in the raffle is a holiday for two in Pairs.
35. Which vintage would you prefer?
36. We're doing a special promotion this week.
37. The highest I would be willing to go is 200 RMB.
38. This is the best price I can offer. You can't get it any cheaper than here.
39. How is the color of the wine?
40. You'll get a free gift if you spend up to 300 Yuan.
41. The price is set. We're unable to give any price reduction.
42. The price is fixed.
43. We can't give you any discount.
44. If you have a membership card of your department store, we'll give you a 10% off.
45. You'll get a coupon to join our raffle if you spend up to 300 Yuan in our counter.
46. How is the taste of the wine?
47. Can't you take a little more off?
48. People from southern China prefer rice wine while those from the north drink white spirit.
49. If you prefer mild liquor, I think the Chinese yellow wine will be a good choice.

Food Instructions

Riesling Wine

The Riesling, also known as the "queen of the grapes" formed the basis for the world reputation enjoyed by German white wines. This Riesling captivates everyone with its youthfully fresh interplay of aromas: ripe citrus fruits, coupled with juicy peaches.

Riesling is a white grape variety originating in the Rhine region of Germany. It is typically used to make dry, semi-sweet, sweet and sparkling white wines. In terms of importance for quality wines, it is usually included in the "top three" white wine varieties together with Chardonnay and Sauvignon Blanc, and is the most grown variety in Germany.

Ugni Blanc Wine

Ugni Blanc grape is famous of Trebiano Toscana. It is from the eastern of Mediterranean Sea, contains fruit's acidity and the light feeling in the mouth, and makes the association of bitter almond's fragrance. This medium-dry sparkling wine is fruity and rich, with a long lasting finish.

Students' Task

Please finish the following tasks according to the given words, phrases, expressions and scene description.

Team work 1

Find out the words and phrases related to types of liquor.
Find out the words and phrases related to feature of liquor.
Find out the words and phrases related to the raw material of liquor.
Find out the words and phrases related to bargain or price.

Scene Four *At the Liquor Area*

Find out the words and phrases related to promotion or sale.
Find out the words and phrases related to way of payment.

Team work 2

Find out the sentences about introduction of the brand, material, flavor and function of Chinese alcohol.
Find out the sentences about bargain between salesperson and customer.
Find out the sentences about promotion and sales.

Team work 3

Make a conversation according to the given scene description, words and expressions.

Team work 4

Role Play: Act out the above conversation.

 Team work record

The members of team

Number	Name	The task of every member	role
1			
2			
3			
4			
...			

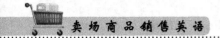

Useful words collected

Useful expressions collected

Team Fruit (Conversation made according to the scene description)

Scene Four *At the Liquor Area*

 **Evaluation**

> The evaluation from teacher

> The evaluation from other teams

> The evaluation from the member of your team

> The evaluation from yourself

39

Scene Five At the Grocery Area

 Objectives

学习目标		
专业能力	方法能力	社会能力
●能说出常见休闲食品的英语名称； ●能读懂休闲食品说明书、配料表等； ●能用英语介绍食品饮料的成分等； ●作为收银人员，能用英语流利地为顾客受理付款业务，用英语帮助顾客完成开具发票等业务； ●作为总台服务人员，能用英语流利地回答关于商场服务方面的问题； ●作为顾客，能流利地表达自己的购买想法，能用英语完成付款过程； ●能用所给材料及自己查找的信息按照要求自编英语对话； ●能够按照自编对话自然地进行情景剧表演。	●能够利用互联网、英语字典、书籍等各种方式查找自己需要的信息； ●能够从各种信息中筛选需要的有用信息； ●能够总结有效的英语学习方法并与同学进行分享。	●能自行完成小组成员的任务分工并共同完成任务； ●能接受他人的合理意见； ●能清晰地表达自己的意见并说服他人接受自己的意见； ●能对他人及自己进行客观真实的评价。
学习任务		
●根据教师提供的场景描述及相关材料，每个小组合作完成情境对话，并进行情景剧表演； ●情境对话中要包含场景描述中提到的内容，同时每个小组可根据需要适当增加情节； ●情境对话中的人物可根据情节需要自行增加或减少。		

Information Bank

Scene description

在副食区，Green夫妇想给他们的儿子John买些零食。售货员向他们推荐了几种比较受孩子欢迎的零食。John挑选了自己喜欢的零食（如巧克力、蛋糕、薯片等），Green夫妇对John挑选的零食是否有益健康表示担心，售货员为他们推荐了较为健康的零食。Green夫妇采纳了售货员的建议并买了食品后去付款。在付款台，Green夫妇向收银员询问是否可以用外币付款，收银员说明如果用现金付款的话，只能用人民币支付，并告诉他们兑换人民币的地方。Green夫妇认为兑换人民币有点浪费时间，决定用信用卡付款。收银员请他们刷卡、输入密码、在刷卡凭条上签字，并嘱咐他们收好小票。Green夫妇在副食区用购物小票换取了食品后，向售货员询问开发票的地方，并去总服务台开发票。开完发票后，Green夫妇向总服务台工作人员询问商场的营业时间（平时的、周末的时间）、洗手间的位置等，工作人员耐心为他们提供各种信息。

Roles

Shop assistant / salesgirl / salesman / saleswoman / salesclerk
Linda
Mrs. Green
Mr. Green
John, the son

Related words and expressions

Useful words and phrases

1. grocery	n.	副食	
2. snack	n.	零食	
3. palatable	adj.	可口的，美味的	
4. invoice	n.	发票	
5. chips	n.	薯条	
6. gourmet	n.	美食家	
7. raisins	n.	葡萄干	
8. exchange	v.	兑换（币种）	
9. receipt	n.	收据	
10. nut	n.	干果，坚果	
11. ham	n.	火腿	
12. puffy	adj.	松脆的	

Scene Five At the Grocery Area

13. sausage	n.	香肠
14. sweets	n.	（英）糖果
15. candy	n.	（美）糖果
16. perishable	adj.	易腐烂的
17. ingredient	n.	配料，成分
18. change	n.	零钱
19. toffee	n.	太妃糖
20. sweetener	n.	甜味剂
21. can	n.	罐头
22. sugar-free	adj.	不含蔗糖的
23. calorie	n.	卡路里（热量单位）
24. lemonade	n.	柠檬汁
25. protein	n.	蛋白质
26. doughnut	n.	面包圈
27. sugar	n.	食糖
28. vitamin	n.	维生素
29. chocolate	n.	巧克力
30. energy	n.	能量
31. starch	n.	淀粉
32. nutrients	n.	营养成分
33. jam	n.	果酱
34. fiber	n.	纤维
35. storage	n.	储存条件，储存方法
36. calcium	n.	钙
37. fat	n.	脂肪
38. coffee	n.	咖啡
39. preservative	n.	防腐剂
40. cookie	n.	饼干
41. carbohydrate	n.	碳水化合物
42. flavor	n.	（食物的）味道与气味
43. cheese	n.	奶酪，芝士
44. assorted	adj.	精选的
45. peanut	n.	花生
46. stuffing	n.	馅
47. mineral	n.	矿物质
48. wafer	n.	威化饼干
49. herbal	adj.	植物的

50. juice		n.	果汁
51. almond		n.	杏仁
52. puff		n.	泡芙，酥皮点心
53. production date			生产日期
54. packaged snack food			包装零食
55. cash desk / cashier's desk			收银处
56. wheat flour			小麦粉
57. processed snack food			加工零食
58. servicing size			食用份量
59. whole milk powder			全脂奶粉
60. net weight			净含量
61. food additive			食品添加剂
62. nutrition facts			营养成分
63. cocoa butter			可可脂
64. skim milk powder			脱脂奶粉
65. soda water			苏打水
66. origin of component			原料产地
67. milk fat			乳脂
68. shelf life			保质期
69. junk food			垃圾食品
70. vegetable oil			植物油
71. foreign currency			外币
72. sales slip			购物清单

Useful expressions

1. Can you give me the receipt?

2. I'm afraid you can't pay with US dollars, but you can exchange your dollars to RMB at any bank.

3. Is the invoice for your business or personal need?

4. I like paying in cash. I don't trust myself with credit cards.

5. I prefer to pay by credit card. It's the easiest way to pay.

6. How much is the candy a kilogram?

7. May I have an invoice please?

8. Sorry, bananas are out of season now.

9. We only accept cash. There is an ATM machine on the first floor.

10. Twenty eight Yuan for the chocolate and seven Yuan for the beverage.

Scene Five   At the Grocery Area

11. That'll be forty seven Yuan in all.
12. Do you use natural, fresh cream in your cream cakes?
13. You can keep the change.
14. Give me a cream birthday cake and two boxes of dark chocolate.
15. How are you going to pay, in cash or by credit card?
16. Can I pay with US dollars?
17. Will you wrap them up separately?
18. I heard coconut candy is a native product here.
19. We don't accept foreign currency.
20. Please step in again.
21. Can I pay by Visa Card?
22. We don't accept Visa Card, I am afraid you have to pay cash.
23. Will you accept Master Card?
24. Please go to the cash counter and pay for it. I'll wrap it up for you.
25. Here are the receipt and cardholder copy, please keep it well.
26. Would you like to pay it in cash or by credit card?
27. We're going to pay by check.
28. Where should we pay for them?
29. Do you take credit cards?
30. You could go to any bank for the exchange of currency.
31. Please invoice for food.
32. You will find what you need here! We have cookies, chocolate, wafers, all popular with kids.
33. This kind of food is fine both in appearance and in taste, and it also has a relaxing effect.
34. Please sign your name on the receipt and keep it well.
35. I'll check the total price for you.
36. As it is after 6 p.m., all of our cream cakes are half price.
37. How late are you open?
38. Don't eat so much junk food. There's too much fat, salt or sugar in them, with little or no nutritional value.
39. What're your business hours?
40. We open from 10:00 a.m. to 9:00 p.m..
41. Chips are high in fat and calories but low in nutrient content.
42. Our basement is open till 11:00 p.m., because we have food departments there.
43. How much do I own you?
44. We don't accept tips, that's our store rule.

45. Here's your receipt and change. Please double check it.

46. Where is the cashier's?

47. There's too much sugar in chocolate and it does harm to your health.

48. What kind of credit cards do you honor?

49. Please give the money to cashier's.

50. It looks and tastes good indeed, but that's because there's too much food additives in it.

Food Instructions

Ingredients: Milk chocolate 30% (sugar, cocoa butter, cocoa mass, skimmed milk powder, anhydrous milkfat, soy lecithin, vanillin), hazelnuts 30%, sugar, vegetable oil, wheat flour, whey powder, low-fat cocoa powder, raising agent, salt.

Net Weight: 260g.

Production Date (Y/M/D): 2011/12/25.

Shelf Life: Best consumed within 14 months.

Storage: Store in cool dry place, away from direct sunlight.

Country of Origin: Italy.

China Importer: Ferrero Trading (Shanghai) Company Limited.

Scene Five   *At the Grocery Area*

Nutrition facts		
Average Value	Per 100g	Per Serving
Energy	546.7 kcal	136.7 kcal
Protein	5.3 g	1.3 g
Total Fat	25.1 g	6.3 g
Saturated Fat	23.1 g	5.9 g
Trans Fat	1.4 g	0.4 g
Carbohydrates	74.9 g	18.7 g
Sugar	14.7 g	3.7 g
Dietary Fibre	0.5 g	0.1 g
Sodium	114.0 mg	28.5 g

 Students' Task

Please finish the following tasks according to the given words, phrases, expressions and scene description.

Team work 1

Find out the words and phrases related to various snacks.

Find out the words and phrases related to nutrients of food.

Find out the words and phrases related to ingredient of packaged snack food.

Find out the words and phrases related to feature of food.

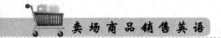

Find out the words and phrases related to payment.

Team work 2

Find out the sentences about buying and selling snack.

Find out the sentences about way of payment.

Find out the sentences about general information or service of department store.

Team work 3

Make a conversation according to the given scene description, words and expressions.

Team work 4

Role Play: Act out the above conversation.

 Team work record

The members of team

Number	Name	The task of every member	role
1			
2			
3			
4			
…			

Scene Five　*At the Grocery Area*

Useful words collected

Useful expressions collected

Team Fruit (Conversation made according to the scene description)

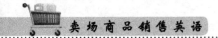

Evaluation

The evaluation from teacher

The evaluation from other teams

The evaluation from the member of your team

The evaluation from yourself

Scene Six
At the Home Appliance Area

 Objectives

学习目标		
专业能力	方法能力	社会能力
●能说出各类常见家电产品的英语名称； ●作为销售人员，能用英语介绍家电产品的使用方法、产品保修条件及配送、安装事宜等； ●作为顾客，能就商品的功能、配送、安装等问题用英语进行提问； ●能用所给材料及自己查找的信息按照要求自编英语对话； ●能够按照自编对话自然地进行情景剧表演。	●能够利用互联网、英语字典、书籍等各种方式查找自己需要的信息； ●能够从各种信息中筛选需要的有用信息； ●能够总结有效的英语学习方法并与同学进行分享。	●能自行完成小组成员的任务分工并共同完成任务； ●能接受他人的合理意见； ●能清晰地表达自己的意见并说服他人接受自己的意见； ●能对他人及自己进行客观真实的评价。

学习任务

●根据教师提供的场景描述及相关材料，每个小组合作完成情境对话，并进行情景剧表演；
●情境对话中要包含场景描述中提到的内容，同时每个小组可根据需要适当增加情节；
●情境对话中的人物可根据情节需要自行增加或减少。

卖场商品销售英语

 Information Bank

Scene description

在家电区，Green夫妇想买一台家电（如电视机、洗衣机、摄像机等），售货员向他们介绍某个品牌商品的使用方法、功能等，并向Green夫妇介绍了商品的安装、调试、售后服务等情况。Green夫妇在听过售货员的介绍后，对商品的功能及售后服务表示满意，并购买了该商品。他们要求商场提供送货服务，并对送货的时间等提出要求，服务员耐心向他们介绍了商场的送货规定。

Roles

Shop assistant / salesgirl / salesman / saleswoman / salesclerk
Linda
Mrs. Green
Mr. Green

Related words and expressions

Useful words and phrases

1. semiautomatic	adj.		半自动的
2. watt	n.		瓦特（电功率单位）
3. recorder	n.		录音机
4. shockproof	adj.		防震的
5. television	n.		电视机
6. install	n.		安装
7. humidifier	n.		加湿器
8. one-touch	n.		一键式
9. refrigerator	n.		冰箱
10. dishwasher	n.		洗碗机
11. dryer	n.		干衣机
12. interface	n.		界面
13. toaster	n.		面包机
14. capacity	n.		容积
15. eggbeater	n.		打蛋器
16. display	n., v.		显示
17. warranty	n.		保修期
18. sterilizer	n.		消毒柜

Scene Six At the Home Appliance Area

19. measurement	n.	尺寸
20. automatic	adj.	自动的
21. reminder	n.	提醒器
22. compact	adj.	紧凑的
23. beep	n.	（电器设备发出的）嘟嘟声；提示音
24. feedback	n.	反馈
25. portable	adj.	手提的，便携式的
26. function	n.	功能
27. test	v.	调试
28. broiler	n.	烘烤机
29. repair	v.	维修
30. plug	n.	插头
31. speaker	n.	扬声器
32. hi-fi	adj.	（收音、录音设备等）高保真度的
33. compatible	adj.	兼容的
34. mechanical	adj.	机械的
35. rinse	v.	漂洗
36. flash	n.	闪光灯
37. electric iron		电熨斗
38. after service center		售后服务中心
39. energy saving		节能
40. electric cooker		电饭锅
41. low noise design		低噪声设计
42. video camera		摄像机
43. child lock		儿童安全锁
44. electric heater		电暖气
45. electronic oven		电烤箱
46. automatic setting		自动设置
47. microwave oven		微波炉
48. easy iron		免熨烫
49. express button		快捷按钮
50. air conditioner		空调
51. water heater		热水器
52. operating instructions		使用说明书，操作指南
53. food blender		搅拌机
54. shortcut key		快捷键
55. electric fan		电风扇

56. electric pressure cooker 电高压锅
57. remote control 遥控
58. water purifier 净水器
59. free delivery 免费送货
60. energy efficiency grade 能效等级
61. LED display 液晶显示
62. home theatre 家庭影院
63. power level 功率级
64. juice extractor 榨汁机
65. imported technology 进口技术
66. water dispenser 饮水机
67. soy milk maker 豆浆机
68. warranty card 保修卡
69. vacuum cleaner 吸尘器
70. washing machine 洗衣机
71. disc player 光盘播放机
72. power amplifier 功率放大器

Useful expressions

1. I wonder if you have delivery service.

2. We offer free delivery for area within ring four in Beijing.

3. I prefer a fully automatic washing machine. It will help me free from washing work.

4. The water heater includes remote control.

5. You will enjoy a superior experience with our product.

6. Within 7 days of the purchase (refer to the invoice date), if the product is malfunctioning, you have the right to refund or exchange the product. Within 7～15 days of the purchase, you enjoy the right to exchange the product. From 15 days to the warranty expiry date, the producing party will fix the problem free of charge.

7. This is an excellent product for the price, considering its appearance and operation.

8. The microwave oven runs very quietly and heats your food excellently.

9. The washing machine is very easy to operate. Many customers like the fact that the timer keeps beeping letting you know that everything is ready now.

10. The electric cooker works great and it is pretty quiet. It also cooks or heats up fast and evenly.

11. The warranty card and the purchasing invoice are the proof of warrantees. Please keep them well.

Scene Six At the Home Appliance Area

12. Consumer reports rated the product really well.
13. This product is performing well according to the feedback from our customers, and I don't notice a difference between it and a more expensive one.
14. It is a very well-designed and well-constructed product.
15. It's relatively quiet in operation and the user interface has a number of nice features, like the one-touch 'express' buttons.
16. How long is this soy milk maker guaranteed?
17. What's the brand of this microwave oven?
18. The delivery will cost you 15 Yuan per kilometer for area beyond ring four.
19. Would you please tell me how to operate this toaster?
20. Are there still any other matters for attention when using the video camera?
21. Could you tell me the advantages of this electric pressure cooker?
22. May I recommend this home audio system? It includes a host machine, a power amplifier, a disc player and a tuner.
23. One of the advantages of the refrigerator is that it has a deodorizer to keep the fridge free of bad smells.
24. Its low noise design reduces the offensive operating noise to a minimum.
25. The washing machine must be installed and operated in a room with the drain.
26. The warranty period is two years. Even when the warranty expires, you can still enjoy a discount on any repair words by presenting the expired warranty card.
27. You will definitely enjoy free delivery and install service.
28. Do you have an operating instruction written in English?
29. It is under warranty for three years.
30. Please read the instructions carefully before you use it. It will show you how to use it safely.
31. Would you like to take it with you or have it delivered?
32. The washing machine is very easy to operate. Just put the plug in the socket, turn on the tap, and press this button. It will begin to work.
33. The delivery is free of charge within the Beijing area.
34. Would you please deliver it to us next Saturday or Sunday? We work from Monday to Friday, and Saturday or Sunday is best for me.
35. Can I specify a date of delivery?
36. The electric water heater has a good quality and is safely to use.
37. How much does it cost for delivery and install?
38. The manufacturer will arrange for a trained technician to install and test it for you free of charge.

39. Would you please demonstrate how to use the camera?

40. When the washing is done, will the electricity be cut off automatically?

41. How long is the warranty period?

42. After the washing program has ended, please remember to cut the supply of power and water immediately.

43. This is the warranty card. Just call the customer service of the manufacturer, their technician will help you to solve the problem.

Students' Task

Please finish the following tasks according to the given words, phrases, expressions and scene description.

Team work 1

Find out the words and phrases related to various home appliances.

Find out the words and phrases related to functions of home appliance.

Find out the words and phrases related to after service.

Team work 2

Find out the sentences about function of home appliance.

Find out the sentences about feature of home appliance.

Find out the sentences about operation of home appliance.

Find out the sentences about delivery.

Find out the sentences about warranty.

Team work 3

Make a conversation according to the given scene description, words and expressions.

Team work 4

Role Play: Act out the above conversation.

Scene Six *At the Home Appliance Area*

 Team work record

The members of team

Number	Name	The task of every member	role
1			
2			
3			
4			
...			

Useful words collected

Useful expressions collected

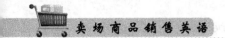

Team Fruit (Conversation made according to the scene description)

Scene Six *At the Home Appliance Area*

 *Evaluation*

The evaluation from teacher

The evaluation from other teams

The evaluation from the member of your team

The evaluation from yourself

Scene Seven
At the Leather Goods Area

 Objectives

学习目标		
专业能力	方法能力	社会能力
●能说出各类常见鞋、包的英语名称； ●作为销售人员，能用英语对鞋、包进行推销； ●作为销售人员，能用英语妥善处理顾客的退换货、投诉等事宜，并能向顾客用英语表达歉意等； ●作为顾客，能用英语说明要求退换货的理由，并能对商场的商品或服务进行投诉； ●能用所给材料及自己查找的信息按照要求自编英语对话； ●能够按照自编对话自然地进行情景剧表演。	●能够利用互联网、英语字典、书籍等各种方式查找自己需要的信息； ●能够从各种信息中筛选需要的有用信息； ●能够总结有效的英语学习方法并与同学进行分享。	●能自行完成小组成员的任务分工并共同完成任务； ●能接受他人的合理意见； ●能清晰地表达自己的意见并说服他人接受自己的意见； ●能对他人及自己进行客观真实的评价。

学习任务
●根据教师提供的场景描述及相关材料，每个小组合作完成情境对话，并进行情景剧表演； ●情境对话中要包含场景描述中提到的内容，同时每个小组可根据需要适当增加情节； ●情境对话中的人物可根据情节需要自行增加或减少。

Information Bank

Scene description 1

Mr. Green在皮具区要买一双鞋，经过售货员的推荐、试穿后选中了一双并买了下来。他回家后却发现鞋的号码不对，于是第二天又带着鞋到商场要求换鞋，并抱怨售货员太不认真，导致他大老远跑来换鞋。售货员对此表示了歉意，并礼貌地请他出示销售小票以证实鞋的确是他们销售的。Mr. Green出示销售小票后，售货员发现的确是自己弄错了，诚挚地向顾客道歉。因其态度诚恳，最后Mr. Green先生表示了谅解。

Scene description 2

在皮具区，Mrs. Green看中了一个精致的女式包。在询问价格并试背后，她感觉价格不贵，样式也不错就买了下来。但是她用了两天后，发现这个包的拉链不好拉，于是到商场要求退货。售货员解释说这款包是处理商品，按照商场的规定是不能退换的。Mrs. Green有点不高兴，她认为在她买包之前售货员并没有说明这个问题，所以导致她没有太认真地检查包的质量，所以她坚决要求退货。在遭到售货员的拒绝后，Mr. Green夫妇向商场投诉部投诉。皮具区负责人过来解决这个纠纷，在听完Green夫妇的理由后，认为售货员在他们购买之前没有说明退换货条件的做法的确不对。经过协商，皮具区负责人和Green夫妇达成协议，为Mrs. Green更换一个同样款式的包，并向Green夫妇表示了诚挚的歉意。

Roles

Shop assistant / salesgirl / salesman / saleswoman / salesclerk
Linda
Mrs. Green
Mr. Green
Head of leather goods area

Related words and expressions

Useful words and phrases

1. backpack	n.	背包
2. logo	n.	商标
3. slipper	n.	拖鞋
4. heel	n.	鞋跟
5. elastic	n.	松紧带

Scene Seven At the Leather Goods Area

6. stylish	adj.		时尚的
7. canvas shoes	n.		帆布鞋
8. zipper	n.		拉链
9. refund	v.		退钱
10. handle	n.		手把
11. wallet	n.		男士钱包
12. boots	n.		靴子
13. polish	n.		鞋油
14. sandals	n.		凉鞋
15. purse	n.		女士钱包
16. ignore	v.		忽视
17. sole	n.		鞋底
18. rude	adj.		粗鲁的
19. exchange	v.		换货
20. briefcase	n.		公文包
21. refuse	v.		拒绝
22. handbag	n.		手提包
23. shoelace	n.		鞋带
24. return	v.		退货
25. cheat	v., n.		欺骗
26. packing	n.		包装
27. reimburse	v.		偿还，赔偿
28. accessories	n.		（包的）配饰
29. tote bag			大手提袋
30. inner label			内标
31. hook buckle			钩扣
32. off-price merchandise			特价商品
33. sports shoes			运动鞋
34. lady bag			女士包
35. complaint department			投诉部
36. casual shoes			便鞋
37. inner pocket			里袋
38. hiking shoes/traveling shoes			旅游鞋
39. waist bag			腰包
40. high boots			长筒靴
41. defective goods			残次品
42. plain toe			（鞋）平头

43. shoulder bag	肩包
44. snow boots	雪地靴
45. leather suitcase	皮箱
46. sharp toe	（鞋）尖头
47. high heels	高跟鞋
48. look into	调查
49. slip-resistant outsole	防滑底
50. leather shoes	皮鞋
51. lodge a complaint	提出投诉
52. suede upper	山羊皮面料

Useful expressions

1. Excuse me, I think you've given me the wrong change.

2. If you have the receipt, I can replace it for you.

3. I'm afraid I have to make a complaint.

4. I'm afraid there's a slight problem with the leather shoes.

5. I'm sorry, madam. I'll get someone to check it for you immediately.

6. I'm awfully sorry for my carelessness.

7. The shoulder bag looks well-made.

8. And if there is anything more you need, please let us know.

9. We do not accept merchandise for return unless items are defective.

10. If the return is caused by the product quality or the mistake from us, you will be guaranteed to get 100% refund.

11. Thank you for telling us about it, sir. I'll look into the matter at once.

12. I'm afraid I cant' exchange your shoes without the receipt.

13. Please calm down, sir. I'll try to help you.

14. I come to exchange the shoes. They are defective. I didn't notice it when I bought them.

15. Sorry, sir. I will solve the problem for you as soon as possible.

16. How about this pair of shoes? You can fasten up the shoelace and walk a few steps to see how it feels.

17. I'm sorry, but we don't allow returns on sale items.

18. It is made of genuine leather.

19. The bag matches your dress perfectly.

20. I'm sorry to keep you waiting so long.

21. Excuse me, but there's a problem with the bag.

22. You can exchange it, provided that you haven't taken off the tag.

23. I'll speak to the person in charge and ask him to take care of the problem.

Scene Seven At the Leather Goods Area

24. I'd like try on a larger size one. These boots pinch me.
25. I wonder if I can have my money back on this shoulder bag.
26. Please relax, madam. I will take care of it according to your request.
27. I ask for return the clothes. It shrank too much. Now it's too small to wear.
28. I have to lodge a strong complaint. The salesgirl was too rude.
29. The purse can hold all the banknotes without folding.
30. The salesperson just ignored me. I can't stand that.
31. I hope to change one bag with exactly the same brand, same design and same size.
32. You'd better put them in a dry and cool place. And polish them regularly.
33. The shoes are a little tight. Do you have a larger size one?
34. I didn't want to spend money on anger.
35. I'm sorry, madam. According to the store rule, we don't provide refund. But you may exchange another one.
36. I'm afraid we can't refund you after it is opened.
37. Product can not be refund or exchanged since being sold.
38. I'm afraid the sole is too hard. Could you give me the one with soft sole?
39. I wonder if the shoes need special care.
40. How can you treat customers in that way?
41. I prefer this bag. The style is fashionable as well as good.
42. Try on this pair. Its leather is soft and bright.
43. Please accept our sincere apologies.
44. What size is this pair of shoes?
45. I want a briefcase that can hold ordinary A4 sized documents without folding.
46. I have to speak to your manager. Your services are so bad.
47. I do apologize for causing inconvenience to you.
48. The bag matches your dress perfectly.
49. I can assure you it wears well and keeps its shape.
50. If it had any quality question, you can have your money back.
51. We offer a 60-days return policy.
52. Your carelessness will make you lose the job.

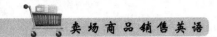

 *Students' Task*

Please finish the following tasks according to the given words, phrases, expressions and scene description.

Team work 1

Find out the words and phrases related to kinds of shoes.
Find out the words and phrases related to kinds of bags.
Find out the words and phrases related to accessories of shoes and bags.
Find out the words and phrases used in the complaint.

Team work 2

Find out the sentences about exchange or return of goods.
Find out the sentences about buying and selling shoes.
Find out the sentences about buying and selling bags.
Find out the sentences used in the complaint.

Team work 3

Make a conversation according to the given scene description, words and expressions.

Team work 4

Role Play: Act out the above conversation.

Scene Seven *At the Leather Goods Area*

 Team work record

The members of team

Number	Name	The task of every member	role
1			
2			
3			
4			
...			

Useful words collected

Useful expressions collected

Team Fruit (Conversation made according to the scene description)

Scene Seven *At the Leather Goods Area*

> The evaluation from teacher

> The evaluation from other teams

> The evaluation from the member of your team

> The evaluation from yourself

69

Scene Eight

At the Gold and Jewelry Area

 Objectives

学习目标		
专业能力	方法能力	社会能力
●能说出各类常见珠宝首饰的英语名称； ●作为销售人员，能用英语简单介绍珠宝首饰的款式、材质特点、保养等简单常识； ●作为服务台工作人员，能用英语处理失物招领事宜； ●作为顾客，能用英语提出关于珠宝首饰的常识性问题；能用英语说明丢失财物的特征等； ●能用所给材料及自己查找的信息按照要求自编英语对话； ●能够按照自编对话自然地进行情景剧表演。	●能够利用互联网、英语字典、书籍等各种方式查找自己需要的信息； ●能够从各种信息中筛选需要的有用信息； ●能够总结有效的英语学习方法并与同学进行分享。	●能自行完成小组成员的任务分工并共同完成任务； ●能接受他人的合理意见； ●能清晰地表达自己的意见并说服他人接受自己的意见； ●能对他人及自己进行客观真实的评价。
学习任务		
●根据教师提供的场景描述及相关材料，每个小组合作完成情境对话，并进行情景剧表演； ●情境对话中要包含场景描述中提到的内容，同时每个小组可根据需要适当增加情节； ●情境对话中的人物可根据情节需要自行增加或减少。		

卖场商品销售英语

 Information Bank

Scene description

在珠宝区，Mr. Green想为夫人买一件珠宝饰品作为结婚周年纪念日的礼物。售货员为他推荐了几款珠宝首饰，Mr. Green 听了售货员的介绍后，对玉饰品产生了兴趣，但是他对玉的了解知之甚少。售货员耐心地为他介绍了玉作为一种特殊材质的特点、中国人对玉的特殊喜爱之情以及各种玉饰品的种类等。Mr. Green听完介绍后，认为玉饰品是送给夫人的理想礼物，就买了一件玉饰品，并请售货员帮忙将玉饰品进行礼品包装。买了礼物后，Mr. Green又在商场逛了一会儿，却发现丢了一个购物袋，他焦急地向售货员寻求帮助，售货员建议他去失物招领处查询那里是否有他丢失的购物袋。在失物招领处，他说明来意，工作人员请他简单描述其购物袋的特征，并详细询问了他最后一次看到购物袋的时间、地点等，最后在失物招领处工作人员的帮助下，Mr. Green找到了他丢失的购物袋。

Roles

Shop assistant / salesgirl / salesman / saleswoman / salesclerk
Linda
Mrs. Green
Mr. Green
Clerk in the Lost and Found Office

Related words and expressions

Useful words and phrases

1. diamond	n.	钻石
2. inlaid	adj.	镶嵌的，镶饰的
3. jadeite	n.	翡翠，硬玉
4. heart	n.	心形
5. bangle	n.	手镯，脚镯
6. ruby	n.	红宝石
7. brooch	n.	胸针
8. carat	n.	克拉（宝石的重量单位；1克拉等于200毫克）
9. stone	n.	宝石
10. teardrop	n.	泪珠状
11. anniversary	n.	周年纪念日

Scene Eight At the Gold and Jewelry Area

12. sapphire	n.	蓝宝石
13. octagon	n.	八角形
14. earring	n.	耳环
15. luster	n.	光泽
16. nephrite	n.	软玉
17. emerald	n.	绿宝石，祖母绿
18. triangle	n.	三角形
19. jewelry	n.	[总称]珠宝，珠宝饰物
20. pendant	n.	（项链的）吊坠
21. leaf	n.	叶状
22. cultured	adj.	人工养殖的
23. jade	n.	玉
24. taper	n.	圆锥形
25. hardness	n.	硬度
26. bracelet	n.	手链，手镯
27. platinum	n.	铂金
28. describe	v.	描述
29. chain	n.	链条；项圈；表链
30. quartz	n.	石英
31. gloss	n.	光泽
32. genuine	adj.	真正的
33. gem	n.	宝石（尤指经切割打磨的）
34. ring	n.	戒指
35. feature	n.	特征
36. constancy	n.	永恒
37. bead	n.	珠子状
38. gold	n.	金
39. missing	adj.	失踪的；不在的
40. ivory	n.	象牙
41. transparence	n.	透明度
42. agate	n.	玛瑙
43. wing	n.	翅状，翅膀
44. coral	n.	珊瑚
45. necklace	n.	项链
46. lustrous	adj.	有光泽的
47. silver	n.	银
48. amethyst	n.	紫晶

49. invaluable	*adj.*		无价的
50. nobility	*n.*		高贵，尊贵
51. pearl	*n.*		珍珠
52. everlasting	*adj.*		永恒的
53. steadfast	*adj.*		坚定的
54. gold plated			镀金的
55. rock crystal			无色水晶
56. jewelry box			首饰盒
57. Lost and Found Office			失物招领处
58. leave behind			忘记携带；遗落
59. white jade			白玉
60. as the saying goes			正如俗话所说，常言道

Useful expressions

1. We have 24K and 18K gold necklaces, rings and earrings.

2. I wish to buy a diamond ring.

3. As the Chinese saying goes, "Gold has a value; jade is invaluable." The Chinese love jade not only for its beauty, but also for its symbolic meaning of nobility, perfection, constancy and immortality.

4. I am really sorry to hear this, but we will try to help you with it.

5. Natural pearls are of higher value, but the cultured pearls have equal luster and just as beautiful.

6. I am sorry, it has not been found yet.

7. Real emerald is always cool to touch and will resist any scratching with metal.

8. Could you show me your ID card?

9. In China, jade is the favored gemstone.

10. Would you mind leaving your name and address in this form?

11. Where had you been this morning?

12. I prefer the crystal to all other gemstone.

13. How do I know the jadeite is genuine?

14. I wonder if the necklace made of natural pearls.

15. These jade bracelets look very elegant. They are inlaid with ruby and sapphire.

16. A flawless diamond is invisible underwater.

17. It is said that wearing a jade bracelet will protected people from illness.

18. What does your mobile phone look like?

19. Please polish your crystal necklace with a soft cloth occasionally. It will help maintain the original luster and beauty over time.

Scene Eight At the Gold and Jewelry Area

20. Can you give us a description of it?
21. You'd better go to our lost and found section to report it.
22. A diamond is the hardest substance found in nature. But it can be cut into different shapes and used to make costly jewelry such as diamond rings.
23. This bracelet is our best. You have a fine eye for jadeite.
24. What is the make of your watch / phone / wallet?
25. The jewels in our shop are all real.
26. This string of pearl necklace is made of over 40 natural pearls that are absolutely identical in color and size.
27. The pair of leaf-shaped earrings is 24K gold and inlaid with emerald.
28. I'm looking for some jewels for my wife as a wedding anniversary gift.
29. May I recommend the diamond ring? Diamond means everlasting and steadfast love.
30. How much is this jadeite necklace worth?
31. This pair of earrings matches the color of necklace fabulously. And they go really well with your skin.
32. May I have your name / telephone number / address?
33. What grade of jade is this?
34. How about this one? This is thinner. And it has a heart-shape pendant.
35. We will give you a call if it is reported.
36. Can you describe your wallet please?
37. Pearls, agate, crystal and jade were regarded as "the four treasures" in ancient China. Among them, the culture of jade is distinctively a Chinese civilization.
38. Don't worry, sir / madam. We'll see to it immediately. If we can find it, we will let you know in the first time.
39. Do you remember the last time you had it?
40. There are two types of jade. One is called nephrite, and other kind of jade mineral is called jadeite.
41. Here is your mobile phone, sir. Please fill in this request slip.

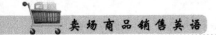

 *Students' Task*

Please finish the following tasks according to the given words, phrases, expressions and scene description.

Team work 1

Find out the words and phrases related to material of jewelry.
Find out the words and phrases related to shape of jewelry.
Find out the words and phrases related to types of jewelry.
Find out the words and phrases related to feature of jewelry.
Find out the words and phrases used in the loss and finding of articles.

Team work 2

Find out the sentences used in the loss and finding of articles.
Find out the sentences about description of jewelry.

Team work 3

Make a conversation according to the given scene description, words and expressions.

Team work 4

Role Play: Act out the above conversation.

Scene Eight At the Gold and Jewelry Area

 Team work record

The members of team

Number	Name	The task of every member	role
1			
2			
3			
4			
...			

Useful words collected

Useful expressions collected

77

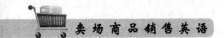

Team Fruit (Conversation made according to the scene description)

Scene Eight *At the Gold and Jewelry Area*

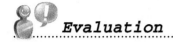 *Evaluation*

The evaluation from teacher

The evaluation from other teams

The evaluation from the member of your team

The evaluation from yourself

Keys

Scene one   In the Wangfujing Street

Part 1   Translation of useful expressions

1. 北京市百货大楼分为北馆和南馆两部分。
2. 谢谢，你真乐于助人。
3. 王府井地区位于北京的中心地带，紧邻紫禁城和天安门广场。
4. 自从1903年东安市场建成以来，王府井大街就变成了北京的一个商业中心。
5. 请一直往前走去乘扶梯。
6. 王府井大街以其百年老字号商店而著称，如瑞蚨祥绸布店、王麻子刀剪铺、全聚德烤鸭店、内联升鞋店和步瀛斋鞋店等。
7. 你们商店明天什么时间开店/关店？
8. 王府井大街上的主要商场有东方新天地、北京市百货大楼、外文书店、丹耀大厦、工艺美术大厦、王府女子百货商厦、穆斯林大厦、新东安商场等。
9. 王府井南口到金鱼口这条810米长的步行街上，林立着200多家商店。
10. 电梯在四楼停吗？
11. 北京市百货大楼建于1955年，是1949年新中国成立以来北京建成的第一个大型购物商场。
12. 这条大街在700多年前的元朝就形成了。明朝时，一位皇帝在这条街上为他的10个兄弟修建了10座宅邸，这条街因而被命名为"十王府"，意思是10位皇兄弟的宅邸。到了1915年，当时的政府将这条街重新命名为"王府井大街"，这是源于在这条街的南边有一眼甜水井。
13. 这里有公用电话吗？
14. 王府井商业大街上林立着各种大型商场、酒店、专卖店和著名的百年商店。王府井大街现在与法国香榭丽舍大街结为友好姐妹街。

15. 北京市百货大楼既是一个可以让顾客轻松买到日用百货的地方，又是一个可以让顾客信任的地方，这是它盛名远扬的原因所在。
16. 我对此早有耳闻。
17. 现在，北京有五个主要商业区，分别是王府井商业区、西单商业区、大栅栏商业区、隆福寺商业区和朝阳门外商业区。
18. 请问我在哪里可以买到儿童服装？
19. 在英语中，"王府井"是指亲王府邸中的井。
20. 百闻不如一见。
21. 我可以从这里拿一本购物指南吗？
22. 王府井大街以其商品的全面丰富、紧随潮流、品质优良以及丰富多彩的文化活动而闻名全国。
23. 在经过五个月的大规模装修改建工程之后，北京市百货大楼于1999年8月28日重新开业了。
24. 厕所在那个角落处，紧挨着收银台。
25. 新中国成立后，王府井地区逐渐变成这个城市的标志性商业中心。
26. 北京市百货大楼以其一流的服务和两千多个品牌下的七千余款丰富商品而享有盛誉。
27. 请问总服务台在哪里？
28. 我们提供手机免费充电服务，您可以在这里为您的手机充电。
29. 谢谢光临，先生。
30. 我们的营业时间是从上午10点到晚上10点。

Part 2　Translation of Store Layout

		北馆
	8层	影城
	7层	时尚餐厅
	6层	家居装饰 生活家电 办公用品 照摄器材 数码产品
5层	儿童服饰 儿童玩具	5层	运动休闲 体育用品 户外用品 休闲服装

4层	男士皮具 精品男鞋	4层	精品男装 休闲男装 男士配饰 户外用品
3层	女士内衣 针织内衣	3层	青春女装 成熟女装 流行饰品
2层	女鞋	2层	成熟女装 女士手袋 流行饰品 时尚腕表
1层	化妆品 国际精品店 黄金珠宝 女鞋 布鞋	1层	国际精品 珠宝 名品腕表 女士手袋 星巴克
北京市百货大楼 Beijing Department Store		地下一层	餐饮 超市 北京特产
		地下二层	餐饮

（参考自北京市百货大楼楼层分布图）

Part 3　Conversation

Mrs. Green:　Wow, we're now in the Wangfujing Street, aren't we?

Linda:　　　Yes, this is Wangfujing Street.

Mrs. Green:　We've heard of it for a long time, and now we're here.

Mr. Green:　It's a so busy street. It reminds me of an old saying: seeing for oneself is better than hearing from others.

Linda:　　　The Wangfujing Street is one of the most famous commercial areas in Beijing.

Mrs. Green:　By the way, what does Wangfujing mean?

Linda:　　　Well, in English, the words *Wangfujing* means the Well of the Prince's Mansion.

Mr. Green:　I guess there is a story about the well and the prince's mansion.

Linda: Yes, you're right. The street came into being in the Yuan Dynasty more than 700 years ago. In the Ming Dynasty, one of the emperors built 10 mansions for his 10 brothers in this street, and the street was then named Shiwangfu, meaning mansions for 10 imperial brothers. In 1915, the government renamed the street as Wangfujing Street, for there is a sweet-water well on the south part of the street.

Mrs. Green: So it has a long history.

Linda: Yes. Since Dong'an Market was established in 1903, the area has become a commercial centre in Beijing. And nowadays, the street is one of the busiest shopping areas. There are more than 200 shops here.

Mr. Green: How long is it?

Linda: The total length is about 1.6 kilometers. It is from East Chang'an Street in the south to National Art Museum of China in the north. But the part of Pedestrian Street is about 810 meter-long from Nankou of Wangfujing to Goldfish Kou.

Mrs. Green: What kinds of shops are there?

Linda: Oh, there are many famous department stores such as Oriental Plaza, Beijing Department Store, Sun Dong An Plaza, Foreign Language Bookstore. Besides, it is also famous for the long-established shops such as the silks of Ruifuxiang, the scissors of Wangmazi, the roast ducks of Quanjude, the shoes of Neiliansheng and Buyingzhai, and so on.

Mrs. Green: Wow, it's marvelous. Where should we go now?

Linda: How's about going to Beijing Department Store? It has a favorable reputation due to its top-notch service and more than 2 000 brands in over 70 000 varieties of goods.

Mrs. Green: Oh, it's fabulous. Let's go.

(In the Beijing Department Store)

Mr. Green: I think we'd better get a shopping guide first.

Mrs. Green: Good idea. Where is the reception desk?

Linda: This way, please.

Receptionist: Good morning. Is there anything I can do for you?

Mrs. Green: Good morning. May I get a shopping guide here?

Receptionist: Sure. Here you are. Anything else?

Mrs. Green: When does it close?

Receptionist: It closes at 10 p.m.. So you have ample time to go shopping.

Mrs. Green: That's great.

Mr. Green: Excuse me. Can you tell me where I can wash my hands?

Receptionist: Wash your hands?

Mr. Green: Where can I find a restroom?

Receptionist: Sorry? A rest…room?

Mrs. Green: Oh, he means a toilet or a washroom.

Receptionist: I get it. It's on the second floor, next to the escalator.

Mr. Green: Oh, thank you very much.

Receptionist: It' my pleasure.

(A few minutes later)

Mrs. Green: Now, let's go shopping.

Mr. Green: Wait. You'd better think about what you want to buy first. It's so large. Do you want to shop a whole day?

Mrs. Green: (To Linda) Oh, he hates going shopping with me.

Linda: Well, so does my husband.

Mrs. Green: OK. Let me see. The store is divided into north wing and south wing.

Mr. Green: We're now in the south wing.

Mrs. Green: Yes. It sells cosmetics, jewelry, women's shoes, fabric shoes and luxury on the first floor. Let's just begin shopping here.

Scene Two At the Cosmetics Area

Part 1 Translation of useful expressions

1. 温和的配方能保持皮肤柔嫩健康。
2. 这香水闻起来不错，我买了。
3. 请问您想买点什么？
4. 您是油性皮肤，最好使用净化爽肤水。
5. 我的皮肤是混合型的。T字部位容易出油，但两颊在秋冬季节的时候却很干燥。
6. 请您再说一遍。
7. 我的皮肤是油性的，脸上常起痘痘。
8. 我想买一瓶美白防晒乳液。
9. 你们卖紧肤液和面霜吗？
10. 你能给我演示一下怎么使用睫毛夹吗？
11. 我不喜欢这个味道。
12. 这款面膜适合干性皮肤使用。
13. 这款精华液是抗皱美白的。
14. 不好意思，您说的"控油面霜"是什么意思？
15. 我想买一个唇膏。
16. 能为您效劳吗？
17. 您介意我为您推荐一下吗？
18. 这个品牌怎么样？这是一个新品牌。
19. 不要长时间一直使用同一个品牌的面霜。
20. 欢迎光临，先生。请您随便看看。
21. 这款保湿乳是抗干燥的，可以使您的皮肤得到滋养保湿。
22. 抱歉，我没有明白您的意思。
23. 我只是随便看看。
24. 很多人都买这款产品，都说它不错。
25. 有什么产品是抗干燥的？
26. 这款乳液味道太重了，我受不了。
27. 您能再重复一次吗？
28. 我们有试用装，您可以试用一下。
29. 我想买面膜，你可以给我推荐一种吗？
30. 这里欢迎任何人光临，买不买都没关系。
31. 我不确定这个颜色是不是与我的肤色相配，我可以试用一下吗？
32. 听起来不错，不过让我考虑一下，然后再过来。

33. 好的，我会再来的。
34. 您能给我推荐几款香水吗？
35. 您最好买这种洗面奶。
36. 不好意思，我不会用英语说这句话。
37. 这些天我脸上的皮肤一直很干，你们这里有保湿乳吗？
38. 我的皮肤很敏感，对很多护肤产品都过敏。
39. 我的意思是你们卖那种不含酒精的香水吗？
40. 这些产品有质量保证书吗？
41. 我的皮肤在冬天总是很粗糙。
42. 什么牌子的晚霜最好？
43. 我想要味道不是很浓的香水。她喜欢味道稍淡的香水。
44. 我觉得您的皮肤是油性的，这款产品就是为油性皮肤设计的。
45. 这款洗面奶能够彻底清洁您的皮肤，但又不会洗去保护表皮的天然油分，而且配方温和，能保持皮肤清爽、光滑、柔嫩。
46. 您能说得再慢一些吗？
47. 这支唇彩怎么样？那种闪闪的效果会使您看起来更年轻。
48. 这款粉底霜选用最好的原料。它可以滋润您的皮肤，同时保护您的皮肤不会受到有害紫外线的辐射。
49. 您最好使用比较柔和的、霜状的洗面乳，而且要记得洗完脸后擦上滋润型的保湿霜。
50. 你们这里有能让皮肤保持柔嫩细致的护肤品吗？

Part 2　Translation of Cosmetic Instructions

洁肤露

　　轻柔配方提供柔润而有效的洁肤作用，其活性泡沫能柔和而彻底地清除阻塞毛孔的杂质残妆。植物精华成分能舒缓晒后不适的皮肤，用后的肌肤柔软细滑且富于弹力。

使用方法

　　取适量于指尖，轻柔打圈按摩，避开眼睛四周，用化妆棉轻抹并以清水洗净。

保湿面膜

专为暗哑干燥而设计的即时补品。只需15分钟，面膜中的妍白精华帮助减淡由紫外线照射引起的色斑，水溶胶原则改善肌肤弹力，天然矿物更大量地提升皮肤细胞中的水分含量，并帮助巩固细胞天然锁水能力，使皮肤变得细白、润泽，而且弹力充盈。

使用方法

洁面后，取适量敷全脸约15分钟，避开眼睛四周，再用清水洗净。

Part 3 Conversation

Conversation 1:

Salesgirl: Good morning. What can I do for you?

Linda: Uh, we're just having a look.

Salesgirl: Fine. Please take your time.

Linda: Mrs. Green, do you need any kind of cosmetics? There are many brands for customers to choose.

Mrs. Green: I think I really need some. (To the salesgirl) What is this brand, Borghese?

Salesgirl: Yes. What a great insight you have! Borghese is a new brand for Chinese, but it is well welcomed since it appeared on the Chinese market.

Mr. Green: Oh, she always likes to try something new.

Mrs. Green: Where are they produced?

Salesgirl: Well, would you please say it again?

Mrs. Green: I mean where does it come from?

Salesgirl: It is an Italian brand. It has several series, such as Spa-whitening Series and Hydra SPA Energy Series. Every series have cleansing milk, toning lotion, facial cream, mask, eye cream, and things like that. What do you have in mind?

Mrs. Green: Oh, I want to buy some cleansing milk, what would you recommend?

Salesgirl: How's about the Cleansing Lotion of Spa-whitening Series? I think your skin is on the oily side, and this one is designed for oily skin.

Mrs. Green: Really?

Salesgirl: Yes, this is the product description. It cleans thoroughly without striping your natural protective oil. The gentle formula keeps skin clean, clear, smooth and soft.

Mrs. Green:	It sounds great. But the smell is too strong, I'm very sensitive to fragrance.
Linda:	Oh, yes, the smell is a little strong. I don't like this kind of cosmetics, either.
Mrs. Green:	Maybe it is not what I want.
Salesgirl:	In that case, would you mind me recommending this brand, Shiseido? We've got a fragrance-free facial treatment cleanser. It is for oily skin, too. I'm sure you'll like it.
Mrs. Green:	Shiseido? I've heard of this brand before.
Salesgirl:	Yes, it is a famous brand from Japan, and is very popular in China. In fact, this line of products is fragrance-free, including facial mask, moisturizing lotion, eye cream, and so on.
Mrs. Green:	I'd like to try the facial treatment cleanser first.
Salesgirl:	I'm sure you'll like it. Here are some samples of our products. Do try them out.
Mrs. Green:	Well, it is soft, and my skin is clean and clear after using it. I want to buy it. Any advice, Linda?
Linda:	Well, Shiseido is a nice brand, and if you feel well, just buy it.
Mrs. Green:	OK. I'll buy it.

Conversation 2:

Shop assistant:	Good morning. May I help you?
Mr. Green:	I'm looking for something for my wife. Her birthday is coming.
Linda:	Oh, it's wise to choose cosmetics as birthday gifts.
Mr. Green:	I think so. But to be frank, I know little about cosmetics. Would you please give me some advice?
Linda:	You'd better buy a series of products.
Mr. Green:	A series?
Shop assistant:	Yes. A series of cosmetics usually have cleansing foam, toning lotion, day and night treatment, facial mask, eye milk, and so on.
Mr. Green:	Oh, I'm a little confused. Would you please recommend a series for me?
Shop assistant:	How's about L'OREAL? It is French brand, and it is well welcomed by Chinese women.
Mr. Green:	Yes, I know this brand. It is famous in our country, too.
Shop assistant:	The Spa-whitening series sell well.
Mr. Green:	Let me see. Spa-whitening moisturizer. What effect does it has after use?
Shop assistant:	Sorry, I beg your pardon?
Mr. Green:	I want to know if the skin will be better after using this moisturizer.
Shop assistant:	Oh, yes. It is for anti-dryness and whitening, it can moisturize and whiten the skin.
Mr. Green:	(to Linda) How do you think about this series?

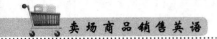

Linda:	The product description says the series are for the dry skin. Are they suitable for Mrs. Green's skin?
Mr. Green:	Oh, I'm not sure about that.
Linda:	It is not wise to choose a wrong birthday gift.
Mr. Green:	Yes. I give up my idea. Uh, maybe I should buy a bottle of perfume for her.
Linda:	That's a great idea.
Shop assistant:	What do you have in mind?
Mr. Green:	I'd like something that's not too strong. She likes softer smelling perfume.
Shop assistant:	Here are three different bottles. Just choose one.
Mr. Green:	Let me see... Oh, I'll take this one. I'm sure she'll like the fragrance.

Scene Three   At the Men's and Women's Wear Area

Part 1   Translation of useful expressions

1. 请问你们这里卖毛外套吗?
2. 你已经说服我买这件连衣裙了。
3. 我想这件衣服的肩部太窄了，袖子也有点短。你们还有大一号的吗?
4. 这件皮夹克你穿很合适，而且它与你的牛仔裤很相配。
5. 这颜色会褪色吗?
6. 这件裙子有点太暴露了。
7. 我需要一件裙子去参加婚礼，你觉得哪件更适合我?
8. 这件紧身裙子穿在你身上很优雅，或许只是剪裁问题令你感到紧罢了。说真的，这种款式没多少人穿起来好看，但你是一个例外。
9. 这是最新的款式，非常流行。
10. 这衣服有点紧。
11. 这件西服是什么牌子的?
12. 这件大衣穿在你身上看上去很不错。
13. 这套西服多少钱?
14. 我觉得双排扣衣服比单排扣衣服好。
15. 试衣间在那边。
16. 我记不清我的腰围了，不过我可以试穿一下，可以吗?
17. 恐怕大号的黄色旗袍已经卖光了。
18. 您想要什么款式的? 时尚款式的还是保守款式的?
19. 您介意我推荐这件吗? 它的设计非常高雅。
20. 广告上宣称打八折的裙子在哪里卖?
21. 这些款式有不同的尺码和颜色。
22. 这件衣服太宽了，你们有中号的吗?
23. 这件运动衣的拉链有点问题。
24. 我穿这件新大衣看起来怎么样?
25. 请随我来裁缝部，他们会为您量尺寸的。
26. 请把挂在那边的黄色夹克衫拿给我看看。
27. 这条裤子是用什么材质做的?
28. 我们的旗袍设计很优雅，款式很有中国特色。
29. 这个颜色对我来说有点太艳了。
30. 设计和材质都不错，但是颜色不适合我。
31. 如果这件白裙子有衬裙的话，我就买了。

32. 我喜欢V型领的，不喜欢圆翻领的。
33. 我们提供免费修改服务。
34. 他们买这件小礼服花了50元。
35. 这种料子可以水洗，而且不会缩水和褪色。
36. 手工艺怎么样？
37. 有些旗袍是专门为身材高挑的外国人设计的。
38. 这些衣服在促销吗？
39. 这件羊毛衫我该怎么洗？
40. 这条牛仔裤要剪短大概1英寸。
41. 洗后会缩水吗？
42. 您领带的颜色与这件西服不协调，我建议您试一下黑色或灰色的西服。
43. 您考虑定做一件旗袍吗？定做旗袍的价格与成品旗袍的价格差不多，但是却更合身，而且手工也精细得多。
44. 这件裙子有其他颜色或尺寸的吗？我需要加大号的。
45. 这套纯羊毛的西装需要干洗。
46. 这件裙子流行吗？
47. 这件衣服腰部有点紧。
48. 这里的外衣种类可真多呀！我都不知道该选哪一件了。
49. 我想买一件黑色的西服，我可以试穿一下这件西服吗？
50. 我喜欢它的设计与材质，但是价格我不能接受。
51. 我觉得灰色不太适合我，这颜色对我来说太暗了。
52. 它可以机洗吗？
53. 这件大衣保暖吗？
54. 您想要什么号码的？
55. 让我查一下库存吧。

Part 2 Translation of Price Tag

零售价

人民币　　　　　　　　　　编号

品名　　　　　　　　　　　单位

产地　　　　　　　　　　　等级

规格　　　　　　　　　　　监督电话

监制编号 Zou-8
价格举报电话: 12358

Part 3 Conversation

Conversation 1:

Shop assistant: Good afternoon, sir. May I help you?
Mr. Green: Yes. I want to buy a gray suit. What brand is this suit?
Shop assistant: Oh, it's 'Gentleman', a very famous brand for men's wear.
Linda: Yes, it is well known in China.
Mr. Green: What's the price for it?
Shop assistant: Here is the price tag. Uh, this suit is 2 980 Yuan.
Linda: Oh, it is a little expensive.
Mrs. Green: I think so. What kind of material is the suit made of ?
Shop assistant: Pure cotton.
Mrs. Green: How should I wash it?
Shop assistant: I'm afraid it must be dry-cleaned.
Mr. Green: Will it shrink after being washed?
Shop assistant: No, it won't. It sells like hot cakes. Both design and quality are good.
Mr. Green: Well, I like the design and material, but not the price.
Shop assistant: It's the latest fashion, very popular. Just try it on. What size do you wear?
Mr. Green: Large size.
Shop assistant: This is the right size you want. The fitting room is over there.

(After a minute)

Mr. Green: How do I look on this suit?
Shop assistant: Oh, it fits you very much.
Mrs. Green: But I'm afraid it's too narrow across the shoulders.
Linda: Yes, maybe extra large size is better.
Mr. Green: I don't think gray suits me well. It's too dull for me.
Shop assistant: I think it's because the color of your tie doesn't go well with the suit. I suggest you try the black or dark gray ones, and I'll take an extra large one for you.
Mr. Green: Oh, no, thanks. It's not too bad, but let me think about it and come back.
Shop assistant: Ok, no problem.
Mrs. Green: Uh, Where are the women dresses that were advertised for 20 percent off?
Shop assistant: Oh, it's on the third floor. Please take this way, the escalator is on the right side.
Mrs. Green: Thank you.

Conversation 2:

Mrs. Green: Oh, how elegant these dresses are! The waistline is so figure-hugging.

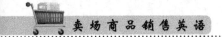

Linda:	Actually, we Chinese call them "Chi-pao".
Mr. Green:	Chi-pao? I heard that before. It is traditional Chinese dress.
Linda:	Yes.
Mr. Green:	Look, there are so many different patterns and designs on them.
Mrs. Green:	Yes, they're so interesting. Do they have any meaning?
Linda:	Sure. Look, the pattern of peony and phoenix symbolizes fortune and nobility.
Mrs. Green:	There're also so many styles. I prefer a V-shaped collar to a turtleneck.
Shop assistant:	Welcome. Are you looking for a Chi-pao?
Mrs. Green:	Oh, we just take a looking. Are these Chi-paos designed for Asian women? I mean for their figures.
Shop assistant:	Of course not. Some are specially designed for foreigners with tall figures. Just come in and choose one.
Mrs. Green:	Well, it feels so soft.
Shop assistant:	Yes, all of our Chi-paos are made of pure silk. The silk is from Suzhou and Hangzhou.
Linda:	The silk of Suzhou and Hangzhou is of high quality.
Shop assistant:	Yes. You'll feel very comfortable on it. Besides, the design is very elegant, and the patterns are very Chinese. They're very welcomed by foreigners.
Mrs. Green:	Well, may I try on that light yellow one? The one with peony flower embroidery on it.
Shop assistant:	Sure. I think the middle size will fit you. Please take this one.

(A few minutes later)

Mrs. Green:	The color suits me well, but it feels a little tight around the waist. Maybe I need a large size one.
Shop assistant:	I'm afraid the size L for the yellow ones are sold out. We only have red ones of this size.
Mrs. Green:	Oh, red seems a bit little bright for me. Are you sure the yellow ones are sold out? I really like it.
Shop assistant:	Uh, let me check the stock. Just a minute, please. (After a while) I'm very sorry, but they're actually sold out.
Mrs. Green:	Oh, it's so pity.
Mr. Green:	Hey, how's about this one?
Mrs. Green:	This one? Oh, it's a little bit too revealing.
Shop assistant:	Well, Would you consider a tailor-made one? It costs more or less the same as the ready-made one. But they are much fitted to the body, and are much more carefully finished.
Mrs. Green:	Really? Can I make one up here?
Shop assistant:	Yes, sure. We offer tailor-made service. Please come to the tailoring department with me. They will take your measurements.

Scene Four   At the Liquor Area

Part 1   Translation of useful expressions

1. 你能给我个更合适的价格吗？
2. 茅台酒是中国最著名的白酒之一，它的味道的确不错。
3. 因为它的质量很好，所以这个价格很合理。
4. 你们接受信用卡支付吗？
5. 这是底价了。
6. 凡购物满100美元即可获赠礼品一份。
7. 我们不能给您降价，这是店里的规定。
8. 太贵了，这简直是抢劫！
9. 葡萄酒是越陈越好。
10. 考虑到质量，这个价钱是值得的。
11. 酒的香味怎么样？
12. 我们现在是清仓大减价，价格打八折，请不要错过这个机会。
13. 这酒度数很高，但是从不上头。
14. 既然您是第一次光顾我们这里，我就在标价的基础上给您打九折，这个价格您不会吃亏的。
15. 我们有低度酒和高度酒。
16. 进口葡萄酒比国产的要好，是真的吗？
17. 这款白兰地酒香味浓郁。
18. 中国的白酒是由大麦、小麦或高粱酿制成的，而米酒是由大米或糯米做成。
19. 这种价钱我不能买。
20. 很多北方人喜欢喝白酒，我想这与那里的气候有一定的关系。
21. 给我一个报价。
22. 茅台酒被认为是中国的国酒。它常常是大型酒宴的必备品。
23. 我想多买点，你不能再降点价吗？
24. 我们简直是在白送人了，这差不多是成本价了。
25. 这款葡萄酒以浓郁的黑莓芬芳为特点，余味柔和，丹宁含量较低。
26. 您可以用分期付款的方式购买。
27. 这种酒非常适合与海鱼搭配着喝。
28. 请给我看看你们柜台最好的香槟酒。
29. 这是公平交易。
30. 这款半干气泡葡萄酒果香浓郁，它蕴含水果般的酸度和清淡口感，令人联想起苦杏仁的芬芳。

31. "雷司令"是德国莱茵河区的一种白葡萄品种，通常用于酿造干、半甜、甜型葡萄酒或气泡酒。
32. 这款"雷司令"葡萄酒以生动清新的芬芳吸引品尝者：成熟柑橘，配合多汁水蜜桃调和而成。
33. 这是中国知名的一种葡萄酒，味道很好。
34. 我们有一个幸运抽奖活动，一等奖是双人巴黎游。
35. 您喜欢哪种葡萄酒？
36. 我们这周正在搞特价促销活动。
37. 我最高出价200元。
38. 这是我能给您的最好报价了。您在其他任何地方也不会得到比这更便宜的价格了。
39. 酒的颜色如何？
40. 如果您消费满300元就可获赠礼品一份。
41. 价格是固定的，我们不能给您任何折扣。
42. 价格是固定的。
43. 我们不能给您打折。
44. 如果您有我们商场的会员卡，我们将给您打九折。
45. 如果在我们柜台消费300元，您就可以得到一张礼券参加我们的抽奖活动。
46. 这酒的味道怎么样？
47. 能再便宜点吗？
48. 在中国，南方人喜欢喝米酒，而北方人喜欢喝白酒。
49. 如果您喜欢温和的酒，中国的黄酒会是一个不错的选择。

Part 2　Translation of Food Instructions

雷司令葡萄酒

　　雷司令葡萄也称为"葡萄皇后"，塑造了德国白葡萄酒所享有的全球声誉。这款雷司令葡萄酒以生动清新的芬芳吸引品尝者：成熟柑橘，配合多汁蜜桃调和而成。

　　雷司令是德国莱茵河区的一种白葡萄品种，通常用于酿造干、半甜、甜型葡萄酒或气泡酒。它和莎当妮、白苏维翁被称为"三种顶尖白葡萄品种"，也是德国最成熟的品种。

> **白玉霓葡萄酒**
>
> 白玉霓葡萄以"Trebiano Toscana"而知名。它来自地中海东部，蕴含水果般的酸度和清淡口感，令人联想起苦杏仁的芬芳。这款半干气泡酒果香浓郁，略带苹果和柑橘香味，余味悠长。

Part 3   Conversation

Mr. Green: Linda, I want to buy some Chinese alcohol for my friends.

Mrs. Green: Why Chinese alcohol? I prefer cocktail or whiskey of our country.

Mr. Green: Oh, sometimes we should try something new.

Mrs. Green: Here we are. Oh, it seems that there is a great variety of alcohols.

Mr. Green: That's great. We'll have more choice.

Salesman: Welcome. Can I help you?

Mr. Green: I'm looking for Chinese alcohol for my friends. Any recommendation?

Salesman: Oh, it depends on what kind of alcohol you would like. You see, we have Chinese white spirit, wine, rice wine, and….

Mr. Green: Wait, wait. What do you mean by rice wine and white spirit? I'm just confused.

Salesman: Rice wine is made from rice or sticky rice, while the Chinese white spirit is made from barley, wheat or Chinese sorghum. People from southern China prefer rice wine while those from the north drink white spirit.

Linda: Yes, my father is fond of rice wine, and sometimes my mother made rice wine for him.

Salesman: You must come from south part of China.

Linda: Yes. I'm from Hubei Province.

Mr. Green: But why do people in different places make a different choice?

Linda: I guess it has something to do with the climate.

Mr. Green: Which alcohol is mild?

Salesman: Rice wine is mild. But why not try Moutai? It is one of the most famous liquors in China and is regarded as China's national liquor. It's often a must for a grand banquet.

Mr. Green: Oh, no. I don't think my friends like spirits.

Salesman: It's rather strong, but never goes to head.

Mrs. Green: Why not buying some wine?

Mr. Green:	Great idea. I think they'll like to try some Chinese wine.
Salesman:	For Chinese wine, I recommend the wine of Greatwall.
Mrs. Green:	Great Wall?
Linda:	He is saying a brand of wine. It is a well-known kind of wine in China. It tastes good.
Mr. Green:	I've heard of this wine before. Ok, I'll take some Greatwall wine. What kind of Greatwall wine do you sell?
Salesman:	We sell almost every kind of Greatwall wine, including different kinds of dry red wine, and some dry white wines.
Mr. Green:	Which kind of wine is more welcomed?
Salesman:	It should be dry red wine. In fact, personally, different wine has different bouquet. It depends on your own choice.
Mr. Green:	Well, I decide to buy 10 bottles of red wine and 10 bottles of white wine. But can you give us a discount, for this is really a big purchase.
Salesman:	Ordinarily the price is fixed, but it happens that we are doing a special promotion this week.
Mrs. Green:	Oh, we're lucky.
Salesman:	Yes. First, if you buy 3 bottles of wine, you'll get a small bottle of the same wine and an opener. Besides, if you have a membership card of our department store, we'll give you a 5% off, and what's more, you'll get a coupon to join our raffle if you spend up to 300 Yuan in our counter. The first prize in the raffle is a holiday for two in Pairs.
Mrs. Green:	Oh, that sounds a good bargain. But we don't have a membership card.
Linda:	Hey, I have the card. You can use mine.
Mr. Green:	Oh, great. You help us save a lot of money. Thank you.
Linda:	And you can try Greatwall wine this evening.
Mrs. Green:	I'm wondering if we can get a surprise from the raffle.
Salesman:	Good luck to you.

Scene Five   At the Grocery Area

Part 1   Translation of useful expressions

1. 您能把收据给我吗?
2. 恐怕您不能用美元支付,但是您可以在任何一家银行把美元兑换成人民币。
3. 您的发票是开为企业用的还是个人的?
4. 我喜欢付现金。我不相信自己使用信用卡的自制力。
5. 我喜欢用信用卡,这是最方便的付钱方式。
6. 糖果1千克多少钱?
7. 请问能给我开张发票吗?
8. 对不起,香蕉不是应季水果。
9. 我们只收现金。在一层有自动取款机。
10. 巧克力共计28元,饮料共计7元。
11. 一共是47元。
12. 你们奶油蛋糕里用的奶油是新鲜的天然奶油吗?
13. 不用找钱了。
14. 给我拿一个奶油生日蛋糕和两盒黑巧克力。
15. 您用什么方式支付? 现金还是信用卡?
16. 我可以用美元支付吗?
17. 可以给我分开包装吗?
18. 我听说椰子糖是本地的特产。
19. 我们不收外币。
20. 欢迎下次光临。
21. 我可以用Visa卡支付吗?
22. 我们不接收Visa卡支付,恐怕您得用现金支付。
23. 你们接收万事达卡吗?
24. 请您到收银台付钱,我来为您包装。
25. 这是收据和持卡人存根,请您保管好。
26. 您想用现金还是信用卡支付?
27. 我们要用支票支付。
28. 我们应该到哪里付钱?
29. 你们这里可以刷信用卡吗?
30. 您可以到任何银行兑换外币。
31. 请开张食品的发票。

32. 您在这里可以找到您需要的任何零食,我们有饼干、巧克力、威化饼干,所有都是孩子们喜欢的。
33. 这种食物的外形与口感都很好,而且吃后有让人放松的效果。
34. 请在收据上签名并收好。
35. 马上给您结算。
36. 因为现在已经过了下午六点,我们所有的奶油蛋糕都半价。
37. 你们营业到几点?
38. 不要吃那么多垃圾食品,垃圾食品中的脂肪、盐或糖的含量很高,却几乎没有任何营养价值。
39. 你们的营业时间是什么时候?
40. 我们从上午10点到晚上9点营业。
41. 薯片中含有很多脂肪和卡路里,但是营养含量却很低。
42. 我们地下楼层营业到晚上11点,因为那里有食品部。
43. 我该付你多少钱?
44. 我们不收小费,这是我们的店规。
45. 这是您的收据和找您的零钱,请您点收。
46. 收银处在哪里?
47. 巧克力里含糖太多,对您的健康不利。
48. 你们收什么信用卡?
49. 请把钱交到收银处。
50. 它的色、形、味的确不错,但那是因为它里面有很多食品添加剂的缘故。

Part 2 Translation of Food Instructions

配料:牛奶巧克力30%(白砂糖,可可脂,可可浆,脱脂奶粉,无水奶油,大豆磷脂,香兰素),榛子30%,白砂糖,植物油,小麦面粉,乳清粉,低脂可可粉,膨松剂,食盐。

净含量:260克。

生产日期(年/月/日):2011/12/25

保质期:14个月。

储藏方法:存放于阴凉干爽处,避免阳光直射。

原产国:意大利。

中国进口商:费列罗贸易(上海)有限公司。

营养成分表		
每份包含有	每100克	每食用份量
能量	546.7千卡	136.7千卡
蛋白质	5.3克	1.3克
脂肪	25.1克	6.3克
饱和脂肪	23.1克	5.9克
反式脂肪	1.4克	0.4克
碳水化合物	74.9克	18.7克
糖	14.7克	3.7克
膳食纤维	0.5克	0.1克
钠	114.0毫克	28.5克

Part 3　Conversation

John:　　　　Mommy, I'm tired and I want to eat something to refresh.

Mrs. Green:　OK. Let's go and find some snacks for you. (To Linda) Linda, where can we buy some snacks?

Linda:　　　Let me check the shop guide. Snacks are sold on the Basement 1.

Mr. Green:　Let's go.

Salesgirl:　　Good afternoon, sir. What can I do for you?

Mr. Green:　I would like to have a look at snacks for my kid.

Salesgirl:　　You will find what you need here! We have cookies, chocolate, wafers, all popular with kids. There are also a large variety of gift packs to choose from. Which do you prefer?

Mr. Green:　John, have a look at the snacks and take your favorite.

John:　　　　Wow, they sell Murray Cookies here. I'll definitely take that. And…and a box of Ferrero Rond Noir.

Mrs. Green:　Hey, John. Don't indulge yourself with so much sweet food. There's too much sugar and it does harm to your health.

John:　　　　Mommy, please…. I'm too tired today and I need some snacks with high energy.

Salesgirl:　　Excuse me. May I recommend Ferrero Crisp Hazelnut and Milk Chocolate? Hazelnut does good to you.

John:　　　　OK. I agree.

Mrs. Green:　That might be a better choice.

Mr. Green:　well, a box of the Murray Cookies, a box of Ferrero Rocher, and four bottles of orange juice, please. How much do I own you?

Salesgirl:　　Here is the price tag. The cookie is 35 Yuan per box, the chocolate is 68 Yuan per box, and the orange juice 4 Yuan per bottle. The total is 119 Yuan. Here is the sales slip.

卖场商品销售英语

Mr. Green: Where should we pay for them?

Salesgirl: Please give the money to cashier's.

Mr. Green: That will be fine. Thank you. By the way, can I pay with American dollars?

Salesgirl: I am afraid no, but you can exchange your dollars to RMB at any bank. There is one near our shopping mall.

Mr. Green: I see. Then I prefer credit card.

(At the cashier's desk)

Clerk: Welcome, sir. Please show me your sales slip.

Mr. Green: Here it is.

Clerk: Thank you. The total of your purchase is 119 Yuan. Would you like to pay it in cash or by credit card?

Mr. Green: Credit card, please. What kind of credit cards do you honor?

Clerk: We accept Master Card, Visa Card and American Express Card.

Mr. Green: OK. Visa Card. Here you are.

Clerk: Thank you. Please wait a minute. Please sign your name here.

Mr. Green: All right.

Clerk: Here are the receipt and cardholder copy, please keep it well.

Mr. Green: Thank you.

(At the grocery area)

Salesgirl: Here are your snacks. Thank you for your purchasing.

Mr. Green: Thank you. By the way, May I have an invoice please?

Salesgirl: I am afraid you have to go to the service desk for that. It is on the ground floor, near the exit.

Mr. Green: I see. Thank you very much!

Salesgirl: You are welcome.

(At the service desk)

Clerk: What can I do for you?

Mr. Green: I'd like an invoice for the food I just bought.

Clerk: I see. Is it for your business or personal need?

Mr. Green: Personal.

Clerk: One moment please. Here is your invoice.

Mr. Green: Thank you. Could you tell me the opening hour of the shopping center?

Clerk: It is from 9 a.m. to 8 p.m. on week days and 10 a.m. to 9 p.m. on weekends.

Mr. Green: I see.

John:	Excuse me. Could you show me the washroom?
Clerk:	My pleasure. Turn right and follow the sign, you will find the washroom just opposite to the counter of pearl decorations.
Mr. Green:	Thank you very much.
Clerk:	You are welcome.

Scene Six　At the Home Appliance Area

Part 1　Translation of useful expressions

1. 我想知道你们是否提供送货服务。
2. 在北京四环内我们提供免费送货服务。
3. 我想要一台全自动洗衣机。它会使我从洗衣服的家务活中解放出来。
4. 这款热水器有遥控功能。
5. 使用我们的产品会给您带来非凡的体验。
6. 自购买之日起7天内（以发票上的购买日期为准），如果产品出现故障，您有权退货或换货。从购买之日的7~15天内，您有权换货。从购买之日的15天起到保修期内，厂家会免费为您处理产品问题。
7. 考虑到它的外观和操作，这款产品的性价比非常高。
8. 这台微波炉运行起来很安静而且能很好地将食物加热。
9. 这台洗衣机操作简单，它的计时器会不断发出提示音提醒您运行已完成，很多顾客都喜欢它的这一功能。
10. 这台电饭锅运行平稳安静，而且能快速均匀地将饭菜煮好或加热。
11. 保修卡和购买发票是保修凭证，请您妥善保管。
12. 我们的顾客对这款产品的评价很好。
13. 根据顾客的反馈，这款产品的性能良好，我认为它与价格更昂贵的一款产品没有什么区别。
14. 这是一款精心设计、用心生产的产品。
15. 它运行起来比较安静，而且用户界面上有许多好功能，像一键式"快捷"按钮。
16. 这台豆浆机的保修期是多长时间？
17. 这台微波炉是什么牌子的？
18. 如果送货区域在四环外，我们将收取您每公里15元的运送费用。
19. 请问这台面包机怎么操作？
20. 使用摄像机时还有什么其他的注意事项吗？
21. 你能说说这台电压力锅的优点吗？
22. 请允许我为您推荐这套家庭音响器材，它包括主机、功率放大器、光盘播放机和调音台。
23. 这款冰箱的优点之一是它有一个除臭系统，防止冰箱出现臭味。
24. 它的静音设计将恼人的运作噪声减至最低。
25. 洗衣机必须在有地漏的房间里安装并使用。
26. 保修期是两年。即使过了保修期，您仍能在任何一家维修点享受优惠的维修服务，只要出示那张已经过期的保修卡就可以。

27. 您将享受免费的送货和安装服务。
28. 你们有没有英文使用说明书？
29. 保修期是三年。
30. 请在使用前认真阅读说明书，它会告诉您如何安全使用机器。
31. 您想自己带走还是由我们运送？
32. 这台洗衣机操作起来非常简单。把插头插在插座上，打开水龙头，再按这个按钮，它就开始运转了。
33. 在北京市区内是免费送货的。
34. 您可以在下周六或下周日送到我家吗？我们星期一到星期五都上班，所以星期六或星期日送货最适合。
35. 我可以指定送货的日期吗？
36. 这款电热水器质量好，使用起来安全可靠。
37. 运费和安装费是多少？
38. 厂家会安排熟练的技术工人为您免费安装、调试机器的。
39. 您能示范一下如何使用这台照相机吗？
40. 衣服洗完后，电源会自动切断吗？
41. 保修期是多长时间？
42. 洗衣结束后，请记得立即切断电源和水。
43. 这是保修卡。只要打电话给厂家的客户服务热线，他们的工人就会为您解决问题的。

Part 2　Conversation

Mrs. Green:　Hey, darling. They sell home appliance here.

Mr. Green:　So, any ideas?

Mrs. Green:　Let's take a look at what washing machine they sell. I really want to buy one. In that way, I will be free from the bored washing work.

Mr. Green:　But we usually send our clothes to laundry.

Mrs. Green:　That's true. But it will be more convenient if we have a fully automatic washing machine. Do you agree, Linda?

Linda:　Yes. I think a fully automatic washing machine is a necessity for a family.

Mr. Green:　Maybe you're right. Let's go and have a look.

Salesgirl:　Welcome, madam. What can I do for you?

Mrs. Green:　I want to take a look at the fully automatic washing machine. What brands do you have?

Salesgirl:　We sell SIEMENS, Little Swan, Haier, SANYO, Panasonic.

Mrs. Green:　Wow, there's a great choice. Which brand do you recommend, Linda?

Linda:　Well, I bought a Little Swan platen washing machine three years ago and it works

	very well. It is a Chinese brand. Besides, SIEMENS is very popular, too.
Mr. Green:	SIEMENS is a German brand, isn't it?
Linda:	Yes. The SIEMENS washing machine has a good quality and is convenient to use.
Salesgirl:	May I recommend SIEMENS XQG80? This is a well-welcomed platen washing machine.
Mrs. Green:	Could you tell me the advantages of the machine?
Salesgirl:	Well, there're a lot of considerate functions such as easy iron, extra rinse, prewash, intensive wash. And you can select these functions according to the amount, soiling and textile of laundry you wash.
Mr. Green:	That sounds great. And any other great designs?
Salesgirl:	Yes. Its low noise design reduces the offensive operating noise to a minimum. And the reservation function design helps to select the end of the washing time.
Mrs. Green:	That's fabulous. Is it easy to operate?
Salesgirl:	Very easy. Just put the plug in the socket, turn on the tap, and add the detergent into this dispenser, put the clothes inside, and then select the suitable program and additional functions, and press the Start button. It will begin to work.
Mrs. Green:	Would you please demonstrate how to use it?
Salesgirl:	No problem. This is the dispenser. And open the loading door to put the clothes in. This is the display panel, and you can choose the washing program and additional functions on it. And here is the Start button.
Mrs. Green:	It's indeed convenient to use. By the way, how much is it?
Salesgirl:	4 360 Yuan.
Mrs. Green:	The price is within my budget. And how long is the warranty period?
Salesgirl:	It is under warranty for three years. The machine is performing well according to the feedback from our customers. Don't worry about its quality.
Mr. Green:	What should we do if there is something wrong?
Salesgirl:	This is the warranty card. Just call the customer service of the manufacturer, their technician will help you to solve the problem. Even when the warranty expires, you can still enjoy a discount on any repair words by presenting the expired warranty card.
Mrs. Green:	It seems they offer a good after service. (To Mr. Green)How about buying one?
Mr. Green:	If it is really necessary for you, just buy it. (To salesgirl)But do you offer any delivery and install service?
Salesgirl:	Yes. You will definitely enjoy free delivery and install service if you live within Five Ring of Beijing.
Mrs. Green:	We live in Wangjing area.
Salesgirl:	In that way, we will deliver the machine free of charge. And the manufacturer will arrange for a trained technician to install and test it for you free of charge.

Mr. Green:	Would you please deliver it to us next Saturday or Sunday? We work from Monday to Friday, and Saturday or Sunday is best for me.
Salesgirl:	No problem.
Mr. Green:	Are there still any other matters for attention?
Salesgirl:	The washing machine must be installed and operated in a room with the drain.
Mr. Green:	Oh, that's really important. We have the suitable place for it.
Mrs. Green:	OK. Let's buy one.
Salesgirl:	I'm sure you will enjoy a superior experience with our product.

Scene Seven At the Leather Goods Area

Part 1 Translation of useful expressions

1. 打扰一下，我想你找错零钱了。
2. 如果您有收据，就可以给您换货。
3. 恐怕我得投诉了。
4. 这双皮鞋恐怕有点小毛病。
5. 抱歉，夫人，我马上找人为您核实情况。
6. 对我的粗心我表示非常抱歉。
7. 这个肩包看上去做工很好。
8. 如果您还需要什么，请告诉我们。
9. 除非商品有瑕疵，否则我们不接受退货。
10. 由于商品质量或我们的失误而导致的退货，您将确保得到100%的退款。
11. 先生，谢谢您向我们反映情况，我会马上调查这件事的。
12. 没有收据，我恐怕不能给您换鞋。
13. 先生，请您平静一下，我会尽力帮助您的。
14. 我来换这双鞋，它们是次品，买的时候我没有注意。
15. 抱歉，先生，我会尽快为您解决问题的。
16. 这双鞋怎么样？您可以系上鞋带走一走，看感觉如何。
17. 抱歉，促销商品是不能退货的。
18. 它是用真皮做成的。
19. 这个包与您的裙子非常搭配。
20. 很抱歉让您等了这么久。
21. 打扰一下，这个包有点问题。
22. 只要你没有把牌子拿掉就可以换货。
23. 我要找负责人谈一下，让他来处理这个问题。
24. 我想试双大一号的鞋，这双靴子挤脚。
25. 我想知道能否退掉这个肩包。
26. 夫人，请消气。我会根据您的要求解决问题的。
27. 我要求退掉这件衣服。这衣服缩水缩得太厉害了，现在小得都没法穿了。
28. 我得提出严重投诉。那个售货员太粗鲁了。
29. 这个女式钱包可以放各种钞票，钞票不用折叠。
30. 售货员竟然对我视若无睹，对此我无法忍受。
31. 我希望换一个同样牌子、同样款式、同样尺寸的包。

32. 您最好把鞋放在干燥凉爽的地方，并且要经常打鞋油。
33. 这双鞋有点紧，还有大一号的吗？
34. 我不想花钱买气受。
35. 很抱歉，夫人。根据我们商场的规定，我们不退钱，但是您可以再换一个。
36. 恐怕打开后我们就不能给您退款了。
37. 商品卖出去后就不能退换了。
38. 我想鞋底太硬了，可以给我拿一双鞋底软一点的鞋吗？
39. 我想知道这双鞋是否需要特别护理？
40. 你们怎么能这样对待顾客？
41. 我要这个包。它的款式既时尚又大方。
42. 试试这双鞋吧。它的皮子又软又亮。
43. 请接受我们的真诚歉意。
44. 这双鞋多大号？
45. 我想买一个公文包，这个包可以装普通A4纸大小的文件而不用折叠放的。
46. 我得和你们经理谈谈，你们的服务太差劲了。
47. 给您带来不便，我表示道歉。
48. 这个包与您的衣服很搭配。
49. 我向您保证它很好穿，而且不会变形。
50. 如果有质量问题，您可以退款。
51. 我们提供60天的退货保证。
52. 你的粗心会让你丢了饭碗的。

Part 2　Conversation

Conversation 1:

Salesman:　　Good afternoon. What can I help you?

Mr. Green:　　I'm looking for a pair of leather goods to go with my suits.

Salesman:　　I think black and brown shoes both match your suit.

Mrs. Green:　I agree.

Salesman:　　What size do you wear, sir?

Mr. Green:　　Size 41.

Salesman:　　How about this brown pair? The shoes are of high quality and will wear well.

Mr. Green:　　Are they made of real leather?

Salesman:　　Yes. They are made of finest cow leather. You can fasten up the shoelaces and walk a few steps to see how it feels.

Mr. Green:　　But I don't like those with shoelaces. I have to take time to fasten up the shoelaces

everyday. Any styles without shoelaces?
Salesman: Yes. Try on this pair. Its leather is soft and bright.
Mr. Green: OK. Well, they are comfortable to wear.
Salesman: Because the shoes have soft sole.
Mrs. Green: How much do they cost?
Salesman: 300 Yuan.
Mr. Green: Well, the price is reasonable. I'll take it.
Salesman: Here is the sales slip. Please pay at the cashier's. And just take your shoes here with the receipt. I'll put them for you in the shoebox.
Mr. Green: OK. Thank you.

(One day later)
Salesman: May I help you, sir?
Mr. Green: I bought this pair of shoes from you yesterday. But after I take them home, I found I got the wrong size. I wear size 41, but the size of this size is 40. You're too careless.
Salesman: Please calm down, sir. I'm terribly sorry to hear that. But would you please show me the receipt or invoice for them.
Mr. Green: You don't remember you sold the shoes?
Salesman: I beg for your understanding, sir. There're too many customers everyday. I can't remember clearly about that. If you have the receipt, I can replace them for you.
Mr. Green: Here is the receipt.
Salesman: Oh, yes. The shoes are really ours. I'm awfully sorry for my carelessness, sir.
Mr. Green: Your carelessness makes me come all the way down here again. How can you treat customers in that way?
Salesman: Please accept my sincere apologies, sir. I promise I'll never make the same mistake.
Mr. Green: Your carelessness will make you lose the job.
Salesman: I do apologize, sir. There're the right shoes for you.
Mr. Green: OK. Hope you never make the same mistakes.
Salesman: Never. Thank you for your understanding.

Conversation 2:
Salesgirl: Good morning, madam. Do you want me to show you something?
Mrs. Green: Yes, I'm looking for a handbag.
Salesgirl: What do you have in mind?
Mrs. Green: I'm not sure, maybe a leather one.
Salesgirl: Just a moment. I'll get you one. We have some smart bags on sale. Here you are .You may try it on.

Mrs. Green: That's nice, but I don't like the color.

Salesgirl: What about this one? The light purple is very impressive. This is an elegant bag with a reasonable price of 120 Yuan.

Mrs. Green: It looks gorgeous, and it's worth the money. I'll take it.

Salesgirl: I will wrap it up for you. Please pay at the cashier's.

Mrs. Green: All right.

(The next day)

Salesgirl: May I help you?

Mrs. Green: Yes, I would like to return the bag.

Salesgirl: All right. Do you have your receipt?

Mrs. Green: Yes. Here it is. I bought it yesterday.

Salesgirl: And why are you returning them?

Mrs. Green: The zipper of the bag doesn't go smoothly.

Salesgirl: I see. Oh, wait. Madam, I'm afraid the bag can not be refund or exchanged since being sold.

Mrs. Green: Why? It's nonsense.

Salesgirl: Because this bag was on sale.

Mrs. Green: Yes, it was thirty percent off.

Salesgirl: According to our store rule, we don't allow returns on sale items.

Mrs. Green: But you didn't tell me the policy yesterday. Otherwise, I would have checked the bag carefully.

Salesgirl: I'm sorry, but we're not allowed to do it. It is our policy.

Mrs. Green: In that way, I have to speak to your manager. Your services are so bad. This is not reasonable.

Salesgirl: Well. Let me have a talk with the manager.

(A moment later)

Manager: Sorry, Madam, I will solve the problem for you as soon as possible. Could you tell me what's wrong with this bag?

Mrs. Green: I just bought it yesterday at the price of 120 Yuan. Your salesperson recommended it to me and I took it without checking it very carefully. But I found the zipper not working well later. That's why I ask for return. But your staff told me the on sale item can't be returned or exchanged. If I knew this, I would have checked it very carefully yesterday. That's her fault.

Manager: Oh, I see. I'm awfully sorry for our carelessness. Please show me your receipt again.

Mrs. Green: Here it is.

Manager: Well, madam. It's really our policy that the items on sale can't be returned or exchanged, but it's our fault for not giving your clear explanation. For our fault, how about exchanging one for you?

Mrs. Green: Exchange one? I'll agree, if you can change one for me with exactly the same brand, same design and same size.

Salesgirl: Yes, we have the same bag.

Mrs. Green: OK. I will exchange one.

Manager: I'm awfully sorry for the inconvenience we caused to you.

Mrs. Green: It's really a lesson for me. I'll check this bag carefully this time.

Scene Eight   At the Gold and Jewelry Area

Part 1   Translation of useful expressions

1. 我们有24K和18K的金项链、金戒指和金耳环。
2. 我想买一枚钻戒。
3. 中国有句谚语叫"金有价，玉无价"。中国人对玉的钟爱之情不仅源于玉的美丽，还源于它是尊贵、完美、恒久和不朽的象征。
4. 很抱歉听到这个消息，但我们会尽力帮助您。
5. 天然珍珠的价值较高，但人工养殖珍珠也跟天然珍珠一样有光泽而且美丽。
6. 很抱歉，目前还没有找到您的东西。
7. 真翡翠摸起来总有凉润的感觉，而且不怕金属刮擦。
8. 能出示您的身份证吗？
9. 在中国，玉是一种备受人们喜爱的宝石。
10. 您能在这张登记表上填写您的姓名和地址吗？
11. 今天上午您都去过哪里？
12. 我喜欢水晶胜过其他宝石。
13. 我怎么才能知道这块翡翠是真的呢？
14. 我想知道这条是否是天然珍珠项链。
15. 这些玉镯子看上去很精致。镯子上镶嵌着红宝石和蓝宝石。
16. 毫无瑕疵的钻石在水中是看不见的。
17. 据说戴玉镯可以使人们远离疾病。
18. 您的手机是什么样的？
19. 请不时用软布擦拭水晶项链，这样可以确保您的首饰始终保持它独有的光泽与亮丽。
20. 您能告诉我们它的特征吗？
21. 您最好到失物招领处报告您的失物。
22. 钻石是自然界中最硬的物质。但是它却能被切割成不同的形状，制作成诸如钻石戒指等昂贵的首饰。
23. 这个镯子是我们这儿最好的。您鉴赏翡翠的眼光真好。
24. 您的手表/手机/钱包是什么牌子的？
25. 本店出售的都是真珠宝。
26. 这串珍珠项链是由40多颗色泽和大小完全一样的天然珍珠串成的。
27. 这对叶状耳环是24K金镶翡翠的。
28. 我想买些珠宝送给我太太作为结婚周年日的纪念礼物。
29. 请允许我为您推荐钻戒。钻石意味着永恒坚贞的爱情。

30. 这串翡翠项链值多少钱？

31. 这对耳环与项链的颜色非常相配，而且它们和您的肤色也很相配。

32. 能留下您的姓名/手机号/地址吗？

33. 这种玉是什么等级的？

34. 这一条怎么样？这条要细一点，它还有一个心形的小坠子。

35. 一旦它报上来我们就会给您电话。

36. 您能描述一下您的钱包吗？

37. 在古代中国，珍珠、玛瑙、水晶和玉被誉为"四宝"。其中，玉文化是我国独有的一种文化现象。

38. 请您不要担心，我们会立刻为您处理。如果能找到的话，我们会第一时间通知您。

39. 您记得最后看见它是什么时候吗？

40. 玉有两种，一种是软玉，另一种叫翡翠（硬玉）。

41. 先生，这是您的手机，请您填写这张领物单。

Part 2 Conversation

Salesgirl: Good afternoon, sir. What can I do for you?

Mr. Green: I'm looking for some jewels for my wife as a wedding anniversary gift.

Salesgirl: Ok. We have various selections. Here are elegant necklaces, rings, bracelets, earrings made of various valuable materials, such as jade, crystal, gold, silver.

Mr. Green: All of them look very exquisite. I really don't know how to choose. But are they really genuine?

Salesgirl: Certainly, sir. Everything sold here is real. And we have very good reputation in this business.

Mr. Green: Can you show me some jewelry?

Salesgirl: May I recommend the diamond ring? Diamond means everlasting and steadfast love.

Mr. Green: Oh, I've bought her one last year. I'd like to choose some other specials.

Salesgirl: How about jade jewelry? We have beautiful jade necklace, jade pendant, jade bracelet, and so on.

Mr. Green: Jade jewelry? Maybe this is a special choice.

Salesgirl: How do you like this pair of jade bracelets? They are made of natural jade produced in HeTian, the most famous place of jade resources in China.

Mr. Green: I've heard that jade is the favored gemstone in China. To be frank, I know little about jade.

Salesgirl: There are two types of jade. One is called nephrite, and other kind of jade mineral is called jadeite. The jade produced in HeTian is nephrite.

Mr. Green: Why do Chinese people love jade?

Salesgirl: As the Chinese saying goes, "Gold has a value; jade is invaluable." The Chinese love jade not only for its beauty, but also for its symbolic meaning of nobility, perfection, constancy and immortality.

Mr. Green: I see. Can you show me other styles of this pair of bracelets?

Salesgirl: How about this pair? They are inlaid with ruby and sapphire.

Mr. Green: They're really elegant. Maybe my wife will like the gift.

Salesgirl: Many of our customers like its workmanship. Besides, it is said that wearing a jade bracelet will protected people from illness.

Mr. Green: It's interesting. OK, I'll buy it. How much do they worth?

Salesgirl: They cost 8 000 RMB.

Mr. Green: It seems expensive. Could you give me a discount?

Salesgirl: Sorry, sir. All of our jewelry are certified and sold at fixed price.

Mr. Green: Ok, I'll take it. Could you gift-wrap it for me?

Salesgirl: Certainly, sir. Your wife is a lucky lady. Would you please go to the cashier's to pay for them?

Mr. Green: That will be fine. Thank you.

Salesgirl: You are welcome.

(Later)

Salesgirl: Is there anything I can do for you, sir?

Mr. Green: Well, today is really a terrible day. I have just lost one of my shopping bags. There are three new-bought clothes inside. What should I do now?

Salesgirl: I can understand how you feel, sir. You'd better go to our lost and found section to report it. It is on the first floor.

Mr. Green: Thank you.

(At the Lost and Found Office)

Clerk: Good afternoon, sir, what can I do for you?

Mr. Green: I have just lost one of my shopping bags, I am here to see whether you collect it or not.

Clerk: I am really sorry to hear this, but we will try to help you with it. Could you simply describe your shopping bag, sir?

Mr. Green: It's a black paper shopping bag. And there are three new-bought clothes inside, one is a purple skirt for my wife and the others are a dark blue suit of mine.

Clerk: Wait a minute, please. Let me check if there is such a shopping bag.

Mr. Green: Thank you.

| Clerk: | I am sorry; it has not been here yet. But don't worry. We will try our best to help you. Do you remember the last time you had it, where was it? |

Mr. Green: I got a call from one of my friend about half an hour ago, and it was in my left hand then.

Clerk: Where had you been after that?

Mr. Green: Toilet and toy department. I think it is still in the building.

Clerk: Would you mind leaving your name and telephone number in this form? We will give you a call if it is reported.

Mr. Green: Thank you.

(After one hour)

Clerk: Hello, is this Mr. Green?

Mr. Green: Yes.

Clerk: This is Lost and Found Office of Beijing Department Store. Our staff found a shopping bag in the toilet. I think it belongs to you. Would you please come to claim it?

Mr. Green: Fantastic! I'll be there soon.

参考文献
Bibliography

[1] 武蓝蕙. 零售业英语[M]. 天津：天津科技翻译出版公司，2006.

[2] 梭伦. 实用服务人员英语会话[M]. 北京：中国纺织出版社，2009.

[3] 梭伦. 实用英语购物一路通[M]. 北京：中国纺织出版社，2009.

[4] 李雪，李铁红，范宏博. 售货员英语口语大全[M]. 北京：机械工业出版社，2010.

[5] http://www.chinadaily.com.cn/

[6] http://www.chinahighlights.com/